WORDS OF LIFE

WORDS OF LIFE
The Preaching of St. Óscar Romero

Todd Walatka

ORBIS BOOKS
Maryknoll, New York 10545

Library of Congress Cataloging-in-Publication Data

Names: Romero, Óscar A. (Óscar Arnulfo), Saint, 1917-1980 author | Walatka, Todd, writer of added commentary
Title: Words of life : the preaching of St. Óscar Romero / Todd Walatka.
Description: Maryknoll, NY : Orbis Books, [2026] | Includes bibliographical references. | Summary: "A selection of twelve prophetic sermons by St. Óscar Romero with commentary"— Provided by publisher.
Identifiers: LCCN 2025034391 (print) | LCCN 2025034392 (ebook) | ISBN 9781626986695 trade paperback | ISBN 9798888661222 epub
Subjects: LCSH: Catholic Church—Sermons | Sermons, Spanish—Translations into English | LCGFT: Sermons
Classification: LCC BX1756.R56 R66 2026 (print) | LCC BX1756.R56 (ebook)
LC record available at https://lccn.loc.gov/2025034391
LC ebook record available at https://lccn.loc.gov/2025034392

Contents

Acknowledgments

I have wanted to put this book into the hands of my friends, family, and students for many years. I cannot count the number of times that I have seen someone catch a glimpse of the incredible life and witness of Óscar Romero and then ask for more. This book exists because of those continual requests for a deeper encounter with this beautiful saint.

Easy access to the writings of Romero has been made possible for many years through the dedicated work of the Archbishop Romero Trust (http://www.romerotrust.org.uk/). The Trust has supported countless initiatives related to Romero and the Catholic commitment to peace and justice, including making available online almost all of Romero's published works in both the original Spanish and English translations. I am grateful for their support for this project and permission to use these translations. Thus, unless otherwise noted, all of the English translations of Romero in this book are from the translations posted on the Romero Trust website. These same translations are published in *A Prophetic Bishop Speaks to His People: The Complete Homilies of Archbishop Óscar Arnulfo Romero*, 6 volumes, translated by Joseph Owens, SJ (Convivium Press.)

My own reading of Romero has been influenced by more people than I can name here. I wrote this book after completing the collaborative project *Óscar Romero and Catholic Social Teaching* (University of Notre Dame Press), an endeavor that gave me the privilege of working with a group of incredible scholars: Kevin Burke, SJ, Peter Casarella, Meghan Clark, Edgardo Colón-Emeric, Leo Guardado, José Henríquez Leiva, Elizabeth O'Donnell Gandolfo, David Lantigua, Michael Lee, Ana María Pineda, RSM, Stephen Pope, Rubén Rosario Rodríguez, Jon Sobrino, SJ, and Matthew Whelan. Many thanks to all of these wonderful scholars who have shaped my reading of Romero in so many ways.

As I was revising the manuscript of this book in the spring of 2024, I was able to return to El Salvador on pilgrimage with a group of ministry students from the University of Notre Dame. That encounter with the people of El Salvador reinforced the firm conviction that we must always remember Romero as one among the great cloud of Salvadoran witnesses. Many thanks to Andy, Francisco, Ana, Gustavo, Rosa, Nicholas, Gregorio Rosa, and others whose lives testify so powerfully to the fullness of the Gospel that Romero proclaimed.

I am immensely grateful to those who read the whole manuscript and gave me detailed and critical feedback. Their suggestions have made Romero shine forth far more brightly. Thank you to Julian Filochowski, Leo Guardado, Matthew Whelan, Heather Christman, Troy Kassien, Emily Plank, and Ulrike Guthrie for their time and support for the project. Finally, I am grateful for the many forms of support offered by the University of Notre Dame. All of my work on Romero has been supported and shaped by the Latin American/North American Church Concerns program within the Kellogg Institute at Notre Dame. And here one person stands out among so many wonderful people: Father Bob Pelton, CSC (1921–2019). Father Bob was always looking forward, always seeking to bring more Christians in the Global North to a transformative encounter with the beauty and richness of the Church in Latin America. I hope that this book can carry forth his legacy in some small way.

Introduction

"Very truly, I tell you, unless a grain of wheat
falls into the earth and dies,
it remains just a single grain;
but if it dies, it bears much fruit.
Those who love their life lose it,
and those who hate their life in this world
will keep it for eternal life."
—John 12:24–25

On March 24, 1980, Óscar Romero delivered his final homily. At the memorial Mass for a simple Salvadoran woman, Doña Sarita, he urged all those present to embrace and live out the message of the Gospel:

This afternoon, dear sisters and brothers, I believe we should not only pray for the eternal rest of our dear Sarita but should above all embrace this message that every Christian today must heartily proclaim.... You just heard the Gospel of Christ: we must not love our lives so much that we avoid taking the risks in life that history calls for. Those who seek to shun danger will lose their lives, whereas those who, for love of Christ, dedicate themselves to the service of others will live. They are like that grain of wheat that dies, at least in appearance. If the grain does not die, it remains alone. If it yields a crop, it is because it dies, allowing itself to be immolated in the earth.

Minutes after he spoke these words, a shot rang out from the gun of a military sharpshooter. Romero lay mortally wounded at the altar and died minutes later.

In the Christian tradition we speak with reverence of the martyrs, of those faithful Christian witnesses who died for their faith (in Greek, *martyrion* means "witness"). These witnesses lead the way for the rest of us, illuminating the path of the Gospel. In his own day, Romero's El Salvador became a land of martyrs. He encountered the powerful witness of hundreds of Salvadoran Christians, of priests, vowed religious, catechists, and ordinary lay persons whose commitment to the Gospel took them down the same path as Jesus to the cross. In particular, these Christians lived a true commitment to the poor, to those Jesus calls the "least of these brothers and sisters of mine" (Matt 25:40). And their witness transformed Romero. They revealed for him the fullness of the Gospel and the contours of authentic Christian love. And, after three years of serving as their archbishop, he became El Salvador's most famous martyr. Soon after his death, the people of El Salvador, by their words and their devotions, declared him *Saint* Óscar Romero. In 2018, the Catholic Church officially canonized him as a faithful bishop and martyr.

One of my own great privileges over the past fifteen years has been to introduce hundreds of students to the life and witness of this contemporary Salvadoran saint. I have seen Romero's witness open minds and hearts as a sort of invitation to enter into a deeper commitment to the Gospel.

In part, this impact flows from the dramatic character of Romero's story. In Romero, we find someone who was profoundly transformed by the call of God and who lived that call to the point of death. His story is one of real struggle, of transformative moments, of growing commitment, and of a disciple of Jesus compelled to preach and live the Gospel to the end. Here we do not find perfection, but we do find great faithfulness that challenges each one of us to follow as we can.

As you read Romero's words in this book, I should warn you of a common experience of my students—an experience that makes him all the more important in our own day. New readers of Romero, whatever their theological commitments, always encounter deep points of contact between his ideas and what they already hold dear. However, if they read carefully, his words challenge them to consider ideas that they had perhaps previously rejected or ignored. With remarkable consistency, Romero holds together what we tend to divide; he proclaims a fullness where we seek a comfortable narrowness. So, as you read this contemporary saint, be warned: your own vision of Christian life will most likely be confirmed in many ways—and you will be challenged to *really* live out what you claim to believe. But Romero will also push you to broaden your horizons, to see and live the greater fullness of the Gospel.

This book originated from a simple request I have received from many students and friends: "If I want to read Romero, where should I start?" There are a number of excellent biographies and theological studies of Romero, and I would recommend them for a fuller presentation of Romero's life.[1] Romero's pastoral letters and other key

---

1. See the "Further Reading" section at the end of this book.

addresses are published in the excellent volume *Voice of the Voiceless*. However, if you want to *feel* Romero's voice and encounter his profound vision of the Gospel, his homilies remain the best place to turn. This was true in 1970s El Salvador, and it remains true today.

Romero's Sunday homily was, as the editors of his homilies note, "an unprecedented ecclesial and social phenomenon."[2] As he stood in the pulpit of an overflowing cathedral in downtown San Salvador each Sunday, thousands more tuned in on the diocesan radio station to hear his words. Many who knew him said he became transformed when he entered the pulpit. From a shy, timid man, he became a prophet who boldly proclaimed the word of God. The deep conviction that the word of God could truly illuminate the world around him guided and comforted him.

Romero prepared his homilies carefully, but he did not write them out beforehand. His preparation started with prayer, a study of the scriptures, and often a review of certain key ecclesiastical texts. He also spent much of the week simply trying to understand the Salvadoran reality all around him: the hopes, fears, and struggles of a suffering people: "As I listen all during the week to the cries of the people and behold so much horrible crime and shameful violence, I ask the Lord to give me appropriate words for consoling, for denouncing, and for calling to repentance" (March 23, 1980). Romero then entered the pulpit on Sunday mornings with an outline of his remarks, a set of passages (biblical and ecclesiastical) that he planned to

---

2. General introduction to *A Prophetic Bishop Speaks to His People: The Complete Homilies of Archbishop Óscar Arnulfo Romero*, 6 vols., trans. Joseph Owens, SJ (Convivium Press, 2015–2016), 1:31.

quote, and details from the events of the week in El Salvador. And with that, he proclaimed the word of God.

This book, therefore, introduces Romero through his *preaching*. But this presents its own challenge. From his time as archbishop of San Salvador (1977–1980), we have 193 homilies that fill six volumes, spanning over twenty-five hundred pages! Thus, the question my students ask has remained: "Where should I start?" The book you hold in your hands is my answer to that question.

Your Journey through This Book

I have structured this book so you can gradually encounter Romero's witness as it unfolded over time. You will find twelve of Romero's homilies, spanning from his opening month as archbishop to his final words at the altar when he was pierced by that assassin's bullet. For each homily I have written an extended introduction, which I hope gives you *just enough* to facilitate a deeper encounter with Romero's words—the homilies themselves remain most important.

It is impossible to reduce Romero's preaching to one or two ideas, but I would suggest two to have in mind as you begin your journey. First, Romero's whole vision of the Christian faith follows what could be called *the principle of the incarnation.* Christians confess that God saves us, not through a simple declaration of forgiveness from afar, but rather through the most radical, intimate, and unexpected solidarity: "the Word became flesh and dwelt among us" (John 1:14). This is the "incarnation" (literally "enfleshment"). Romero insisted again and again that the incarnation was the key, underlying reality and logic of authentic Christianity. In this book, you will hear Romero's repeated call to his people to "incarnate" the message of the Gospel, that is, to give flesh to the word of God in their lives. This call took many forms: words of consolation, hope, denunciation, and encouragement, all of which were ultimately a call to turn back to God and enflesh the Gospel in one's life. Second, much of Romero's preaching comes down to an attempt to help his people see and respond to their own *human dignity* and the dignity of those around them: "Let us learn to live our true dignity as children of God!" (August 15, 1977). This was his message to both poor and rich; it was his message to those who suffered and those who were committing great atrocities. It is the deep marrow of everything he preached.

The first four homilies, from March to June of 1977, will introduce you to the historical context and central themes of Romero's preaching. I will name some of these themes (such as the incarnation and human dignity), but I will also let you discover others as they come. My goal is to help you encounter Romero's preaching without my simply telling you what you will find. Then, with the fifth homily, from January 15, 1978, I will offer a sort of synthesis of his preaching. This will set the foundation for the remainder of the book: seven additional homilies that take you through Romero's powerful vision of the mission of the Church as well as the final months of his life.

At the heart of this book is a simple conviction: Romero's preaching represents a tremendous gift of the Spirit to our Church and our world today. I invite you to read these homilies slowly and prayerfully. Consider each one an invitation to reflect on what it means to be a disciple of Jesus and what it means to be a faithful Church today.

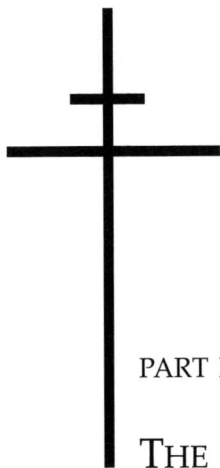

PART I

The New Archbishop

The Motivation of Love

Funeral Mass of Rutilio Grande,
Manuel Solórzano, and Nelson Lemus

(March 14, 1977)

On March 14, 1977, Óscar Romero stood to deliver his homily in the presence of the bodies of Father Rutilio Grande, SJ, Manuel Solórzano, and Nelson Lemus. These three Salvadorans had been killed two days earlier in a military-style ambush as they went to celebrate Mass in the small town of Aguilares. Father Grande was a close friend of Romero's. He served as the master of ceremonies at Romero's episcopal ordination in 1970 and remained a close friend even as other priests of the archdiocese were wary and skeptical of Romero. The elderly Manuel and teenager Nelson were active lay Catholics accompanying Father Grande, and, like so many others, were innocent victims of the repressive violence unleashed by the Salvadoran military. As he looked from the pulpit at the bodies of Rutilio, Manuel, and Nelson, Romero knew what he wanted to say.

But, just two days earlier, on March 12, Romero had stood devastated and speechless. At the news of the attack, Romero went immediately to Aguilares. Before the bodies, he stood in silence for a long while. He knew Rutilio Grande was a faithful priest whose concrete commitment to the poor reflected the truth of the Gospel. Romero listened to the people of Aguilares as they spoke of Father Grande's work and their trust that Jesus would continue to be with them. He prayed in the adoration chapel. That evening was one of many moments of ongoing conversion in the life of Romero. It confirmed a path of transformation that he had been walking for many years, a path that would lead him to his own death three years later.

Romero was born on August 15, 1917, in the small town of Ciudad Barrios near the border of El Salvador and Honduras.[1] He grew up in a simple home, which had no electricity or running water, with his mother, father, and six siblings. His father's steady work as the town's telegraphist offered the family modest financial stability, and they were able to support Romero's education through age twelve. From childhood, Romero displayed a deep piety. He would regularly stop by a church to pray after a day apprenticing as a carpenter, and from a young age he wanted to become a priest. In 1930, at the age of thirteen, Romero entered the minor seminary in San Miguel.

After graduation he enrolled in the national seminary in San Salvador and then went on to study in Rome in 1937. He received a degree in theology in 1941 and was ordained a priest in 1942. He then began a dissertation focused on mystical theology but was called back to El Salvador in 1943 to begin his pastoral ministry. He was twenty-six years old. After a few months as pastor of a small rural parish, his

---

1. The biographical and historical events described in this book can be found in many sources. In most cases, I have confirmed specific dates and details in James Brockman's influential biography, *Romero: A Life* (Orbis Books, 1989).

bishop moved him to San Miguel to serve in an administrative role for the diocese and as pastor at the cathedral. In 1967, he was named secretary-general of the national bishops' conference and moved to San Salvador. There he lived at the seminary, assumed the directorship of the diocesan newspaper, and took on a wide variety of administrative and pastoral responsibilities. In 1970, he was named auxiliary bishop of San Salvador.

The early 1970s were a tumultuous time in El Salvador. Salvadoran society had been marked by extreme inequality and political repression for decades. In the late nineteenth century, land was confiscated from indigenous communities and consolidated into large plantations, mostly for growing coffee. Salvadoran life became defined by an oligarchic economic structure. As one report from 1930 summarized, "Roughly ninety percent of the wealth of the country is held by about one half of one percent of the population. Thirty or forty families own nearly everything in the country. They live in almost regal splendor with many attendants, send their children to Europe or the United States to be educated, and spend money lavishly (on themselves). The rest of the population has practically nothing."[2] This basic structure continued for decades. After a 1932 indigenous uprising was brutally and systematically crushed (in what was remembered as *la matanza*, "the massacre"), the military took over the government and worked closely with the economic elite to preserve their power and wealth. By the 1960s, they employed clandestine groups in the

---

2. Quoted in Matt Eisenbrandt, *Assassination of a Saint: The Plot to Murder Óscar Romero and the Quest to Bring His Killers to Justice* (University of California Press, 2017), 26. For one helpful historical overview, see James Dunkerley, "El Salvador since 1930," in *The Cambridge History of Latin America* (Cambridge University Press, 1990).

countryside to report and suppress movements for reform and, in particular, any inklings of communism. The 1960s and 1970s were also marked by fraudulent elections that maintained military rule.

Despite these repressive measures, by 1970 workers' unions and other reform movements intensified their efforts to demand change. Starting in the 1950s and 1960s, everyday Catholics began to gather in base communities to read and reflect together on the word of God and to form worker cooperatives. The teachings of Vatican II (1962–1965) and the Latin American Bishops' Conference at Medellín, Colombia (1968) further inspired and supported these efforts.[3] An encounter with the word and with one another transformed thousands. As one community reflected: "Our encounter with the Bible was like an earthquake; it moved everything around, it changed our ways of thinking and doing things. It was the first breath that turned the coals red. And in what seemed to be only ash, a fire was born."[4] Throughout this time, Salvadoran *campesinos*—rural farm workers or peasants—found their own voice and felt their own responsibility to live out the Gospel.

One of the main leaders in this movement was Father Rutilio Grande. He worked with the people of Aguilares to help them awaken to the call of the Gospel and read their society in light of the word of God. As he would proclaim to the people, "God is not in the clouds, reclining in a hammock, God is active and desires you to build the kingdom

---

3. I describe Vatican II and Medellín in more detail in the introduction to the third homily in this book on page 33.

4. Quotation from Elizabeth O'Donnell Gandolfo and Laurel Marshall Potter, *Re-Membering the Reign of God: The Decolonial Witness of El Salvador's Church of the Poor* (Lexington Books, 2022), 83.

of God here on earth."[5] The irruption of the poor within the Church of El Salvador was profound and transformative. Supported by many priests and religious such as Father Grande, thousands trained as catechists and "delegates of the word," as persons commissioned to lead Bible studies and communal prayer. And, inspired by the Gospel, they began to question and protest the structures that dominated much of Salvadoran life.

Romero was ambivalent in the face of many of these developments. He had long supported demands for just wages and organizing efforts among *campesinos*, and he was known for his charitable endeavors that alleviated the suffering of the poor. Romero was particularly dedicated to assisting those in the grip of alcoholism, an addiction he saw destroying lives and families. However, when leading priests, religious, and laypersons gathered for the national "pastoral week" in 1970, Romero was largely absent. In part he simply wasn't involved in many of the new pastoral methods and, indeed, was wary and critical of certain dimensions of the movement. He publicly challenged priests and educational initiatives that struck him as too radical, as focusing too much on political issues. He saw the specter of Marxism and its infiltration into the Church as a major issue. Although it would be unfair to see him as a spokesperson for the oligarchy, his overriding concerns regarding an over-politicization of the Gospel often aligned him with their interests. Thus, when Archbishop Chávez retired in 1976 and the papal nuncio consulted with various parties about his replacement, it was no surprise that Romero was the choice of the rich and the powerful. And to

---

5. Quoted in Gandolfo and Potter, *Re-Membering the Reign of God*, 80. Grande said some version of this line many times in his preaching.

the disappointment of the majority of the priests in the archdiocese, he was named and installed as archbishop in February 1977).

Yet Romero had already begun to change. From 1974 to 1976, Romero was not in San Salvador. Instead, during these three years he was bishop of a rural diocese in the eastern section of the country, Santiago de María. After two decades of service as a diocesan administrator, seminary director, and diocesan newspaper editor, these years put him back in a more direct pastoral role. They also transformed Romero. As he traveled his diocese, he saw the suffering of his people. He encountered *campesinos* forced to move from plantation to plantation for poor wages and without a place to sleep; he saw the malnutrition, the lack of health care, and the poor access to education that dominated the countryside; and he witnessed the intense repression that followed in response to even small and peaceful demonstrations for change. Romero certainly tried to respond to the suffering of his people—for example, by opening church buildings overnight to give people a place to sleep—but just as important for his journey was how these experiences were opening his eyes to the truth of Salvadoran reality. He encountered a people filled with faith and hope, but also a suffering people rightfully demanding structural change in Salvadoran society.

Then came the death of Rutilio Grande just three weeks into Romero's time as archbishop. A Jesuit priest, Father Grande had served for many years at the national seminary, and in the early 1970s was named pastor of the small town of Aguilares, just north of San Salvador. In that role, he became a leading figure in the archdiocese in implementing the new pastoral methods among the poor and marginalized in El Salvador. He was also one of the only priests who was friends with Romero, and his death had a profound impact on the archbishop. If Romero's increased contact with the poor in Santiago de María had begun a transformation, the death of Grande accelerated it and defined his path going forward.

Two months later, the rich and powerful spoke of being "betrayed" by the man they had supported to become archbishop. On the other side, many of the clergy and the poor celebrated the change they saw in their archbishop. Important for understanding this transformation are Romero's own words, which we have from two exchanges with other Church leaders. In a letter explaining himself to Cardinal Baggio, the Vatican's then Secretary of State, Romero wrote, "What happened in my priestly life, I have tried to explain to myself, is an evolution of the same desire I have always had to be faithful to what God asks from me."[6] He gave a second explanation to Father César Jérez, the Jesuit provincial superior of Central America. Here Romero pointed to a longer journey of transformation in which the death of Father Grande was but one important moment. Father Jérez recalls Romero as saying:

> It's just that we all have our roots, you know.... I was born into a poor family. I've suffered hunger. I know what it's like to work from the time you're a little kid.... When I went to seminary and started my studies, and then they sent me to finish studying here in Rome, I spent years and years absorbed in my books, and I started to forget about where I came from. I started creating another world. When

---

6. Quoted in James Brockman, *Romero: A Life* (Orbis Books, 1989), 128.

I went back to El Salvador, they made me the Bishop's secretary in San Miguel. I was a parish priest for 23 years there, but I was still buried under paperwork.... Then they sent me to Santiago de María [in 1974], and I ran into extreme poverty again. Those children that were dying just because of the water they were drinking, those campesinos killing themselves in the harvest.... You know Father, when a piece of charcoal has already been lit once, you don't have to blow on it much to get it to flame up again. And everything that happened to us when I got to the archdiocese, and what happened to Father Grande and all... it was a lot. You know how much I admired him. When I saw Rutilio dead, I thought, 'If they killed him for what he was doing, it's my job to go down that same path.[7]

What path did Óscar Romero, Rutilio Grande, and thousands of other faithful Salvadoran Christians take? What can we learn from them today? These questions are at the heart of this book. Standing before the bodies of Father Rutilio Grande, Manuel Solórzano, and Nelson Lemus on Monday, March 14, 1977, Romero gave his initial answer.

For this first homily, I do not want to name its key themes in advance; instead, I want you to encounter it on your own. What would you say in such a moment? What sources would you draw upon for inspiration? I encourage you to read this homily slowly and prayerfully, knowing that in this moment Romero proclaimed much of what would guide his ministry and preaching over the next three

---

7. Quoted in María López Vigil, *Monseñor Romero: Memories in Mosaic* (Orbis Books, 2013), 109.

years. It contains the seeds of ideas that would develop and mature in response to the increasing conflict around him, seeds of the ideas that you will encounter throughout this book.

Suggestions for Further Reading

The themes from this homily reverberate throughout all of Romero's preaching. However, Romero focuses directly upon the witness of Father Grande in two subsequent homilies in particular:

- "The Path of the Beatitudes" (November 1, 1977) in *A Prophetic Bishop Speaks to His People: The Complete Homilies of Archbishop Óscar Arnulfo Romero*, 6 vols., trans. Joseph Owens, SJ (Convivium Press, 2015–2016), 1.401–407.

- "Rutilio Grande: Man, Christian, and Priest" (March 5, 1978) in *A Prophetic Bishop Speaks*, 2.290–96.

Most excellent representative of His Holiness the pope, dear brother bishops, priests, and faithful.

It seems to me that on some occasions, like this morning, the cathedral becomes the sign of the universal Church. It is here that the whole rich pastoral ministry of a local Church is gathered together and joined to the pastoral ministry of all the dioceses of our country and the whole world. We feel that the presence not only of the living but of these three deceased persons gives this image of the Church a dimension of openness to the Absolute, to the Infinite, to the One Beyond: the universal Church, the Church beyond history, the Church beyond human life.

If this were an ordinary funeral, I would speak here, my dear sisters and brothers, about the human and personal relationship that I shared with Father Rutilio Grande, whom I consider a brother. At very critical moments in my life, he was very close to me, and I will never forget his gestures of friendship. But this is not the time to speak about personal feelings but to proclaim, in the presence of these bodies, a message for all of us who continue the pilgrimage of life.

I want to base my message on the words of the pope, present here in his representative, the nuncio, whom I thank because he gives our Church a sense of unity. During these tragic hours, I am feeling this sense of unity in the archdiocese as a hurried blossoming of these sacrifices that the Church is offering. The message of Paul VI, when he speaks to us about evangelization,[1] provides us with guidelines for understanding Rutilio Grande. What does the Church contribute to this universal struggle for liberation from so much misery? The pope reminds us that in the 1974 Synod the voices of the world's bishops, especially bishops from the Third World, lamented the anguish of those who "remain on the margin of life, suffering from famine, chronic disease, illiteracy, poverty" (*Evangelii Nuntiandi* 30). The Church cannot be absent from this struggle for liberation; its presence in this struggle to lift up and dignify human beings must be a very original message—a very unique way of being present that the world may not understand but that provides the seed and the promise of victory and success. The pope declares: "The Church is providing these Christian 'liberators' with the inspiration of faith, the motivation of fraternal love, a social teaching which the true Christian cannot ignore and which he must make the foundation of his wisdom and of his experience in order to translate it concretely into forms of action, participation, and commitment" (*Evangelii Nuntiandi* 38). This is the liberation that the Church proclaims. For this reason the pope states that the Church's liberation "cannot be confused with other liberation movements that lack supernatural

---

1. Throughout this homily, Romero references Paul VI's apostolic exhortation on evangelization in the modern world, *Evangelii Nuntiandi* (December 1975). Romero loved this text, referenced it often, and encouraged others to do the same. Indeed, in August of 1977, when he was seeking greater unity of mission in the archdiocese, he gathered his priests and other pastoral leaders for a three-day study of *Evangelii Nuntiandi* so that they could all go forward on the same, solid foundation.

and spiritual horizons" (*Evangelii Nuntiandi* 33) and especially the inspiration of faith.

The Inspiration of Faith

Here before us today is Father Rutilio Grande, a priest, a Christian who at the time of his baptism and priestly ordination made a profession of faith: "I believe in God the Father, revealed by Christ his Son who loves us and invites us to love. I believe in a Church that is a sign of the presence of God's love in the world, where men and women extend their hands and encounter one another as sisters and brothers."[2] This is an illumination of faith that distinguishes Christians from any liberation of a purely political, economic, or worldly sort, and from any liberation that does not move beyond this world's ideologies, interests, and realities. My sisters and brothers, no one here present should ever think that this gathering around Father Grande's body is some political act with sociological or economic implications. By no means; rather, it is a gathering in faith, a faith that through Father Grande's body, dead in hope, is opened to eternal horizons.

The liberation that Father Grande preached is inspired by faith, a faith that speaks to us about eternal life, a faith that he, with his face raised toward heaven and accompanied by two *campesinos*, offered up in its totality and perfection. It is liberation which culminates in happiness with God, liberation which begins from repentance for sin, liberation based on Christ, the only saving power. This is the liberation that Father Rutilio Grande preached, and he has therefore lived the Church's message.

---

2. An adaptation of the profession of faith from the Rite for Baptism.

The Social Teaching of the Church

First of all, the Church is providing us with Christian liberators inspired by faith. Second, the Church is providing us with men and women who base their lives on a doctrine, the social doctrine of the (*Evangelii Nuntiandi* 38), which tells people that the Christian religion is not one-dimensional, spiritualistic, unmindful of the misery that surrounds them. Rather, our religion beholds God and from the perspective of God sees the neighbor as brother or sister and becomes aware that "what you did for one of these least brothers or sisters of mine, you did for me" (Matt 25:40). I hope that all the movements active in social matters are aware of this doctrine. If they are, they will avoid failure and the short-sightedness that is unable to see beyond worldly realities and temporal structures. As long as our hearts are not converted, as long as our lives are not based on this doctrine that is enlightened by faith to help us to harmonize our hearts with the heart of God, then everything will be feeble, revolutionary, passing, and violent. None of these things is Christian. What gives true life is the social doctrine that the Church proposes to people. How enlightened the world would be if all of us took the social doctrine of the Church as the basis of our social action, our existence, and our concrete commitments in political and economic affairs! This is what Father Rutilio Grande preached. And because this doctrine is often misunderstood, even murderously, that is why Father Rutilio Grande died. He died because the social doctrine of the Church is confused with the political doctrines that disturb the world. The Church's social doctrine is often slandered as subversive, like other things far removed from the prudence which the Church's doctrine posits at the basis of existence.

My brother priests, this message of Father Rutilio Grande is extremely important for us. Let us embrace it, and in the light of this doctrine and this faith let us work together. Let us not be separated by wildly dangerous ideologies, by ideologies that are not inspired in the faith of the Gospel. Let us illuminate our doctrine, our actions as Good Samaritans, and our preaching of Christ's commandment with the light which the Church, as depository of the faith, is trying to make present in these mysterious, convulsive times of our country. This is the message that the bishops of El Salvador proclaimed yesterday.[3]

I am happy, dear priests, for the fruits of this death we lament and of the other difficult circumstances at this moment: the clergy are united with their bishop, and the faithful understand that the light of faith leads us along paths that are quite distinct from other ideologies that are not of the Church, for the Church offers a third way—a motivation of love.

The Motivation of Love

We speak of the motivation of love, sisters and brothers. There should be no feeling of vengeance among us (*Evangelii Nuntiandi* 38). As the bishops stated yesterday, we do not raise our voice for revenge. We are concerned about the things of God who commands us to love him above all things and to love others as we love ourselves (Mark 12:30–31). Yes, it is true that we have asked the authorities to investigate this criminal act, for they have in their hands the instruments

---

3. "Message of the Conference of Bishops of El Salvador on the Reality Facing the Country," in *Orientación* (March 20, 1977). Throughout Romero's preaching he would reference editorials and official pronouncements published in *Orientación*, the weekly archdiocesan newspaper.

of this nation's justice, and they must clarify this situation. We are not accusing anyone, nor are we making judgments beforehand. We hope to hear the voice of an impartial justice because, even with the motivation of love, justice cannot be absent. There can be no true peace and no true love that is based on injustice or violence or intrigue.

True love is what moved Father Rutilio Grande as he died with the two *campesinos* at his side. That is how the Church loves. She dies with them, and with them she presents herself to heaven's transcendence, for she loves them. And it is significant that Father Grande was gunned down precisely when he was traveling to impart to his people the message of the Mass and salvation. A priest was with his *campesinos*, on his way to meet his people, to identify himself with them, to live with them—this was an inspiration of love and not revolution.

It is precisely because it is love that inspires us, sisters and brothers, that we want to tell those responsible that we love them. Who knows if those who are responsible for this criminal act (and therefore excommunicated) are hearing these words on a radio there in their hideout and in their conscience? We want to tell them, "Brother criminals, we love you, and we ask God to pour forth repentance into your hearts because the Church is incapable of hatred; the Church has no enemies." Her only enemies are those who declare themselves as such. But even these she loves, and like the dying Jesus she says, "Father, forgive them for they know not what they do" (Luke 23:34).

The love of God inspired the actions of Father Rutilio. Dear priests, let us embrace this precious heritage. Those of us who heard Father Rutilio and shared his ideals know that he was incapable of preaching hatred; he was incapable of stirring up violence. Perhaps that is why God chose him for this martyrdom: because all those who knew him are well aware that he never uttered any call to violence, vengeance, or hatred. He died loving, and without a doubt, when he felt those first impacts that brought him death, he was able to say as Christ did, "Father, forgive them for they know not what they do."

My dear sisters and brothers, in the name of the archdiocese I want to thank these collaborators of Christian liberation, Father Grande and his two companions, now on the journey to eternity. They are helping us understand the true dimensions of our mission as Church. As we gather now with all our beloved priests of other dioceses, in union with the Holy Father who is present through the nuncio, let us never forget this. We are a pilgrim Church, exposed to misunderstanding and persecution, but we are a Church that walks calmly because we carry within us this power of love.

Dear people of El Salvador, at this crossroad in our history there may seem to be no peaceful solution, and some feel they must resort to violent means. But I tell you, my sisters and brothers, blessed be God who through the death of Father Grande is telling the Church: Yes, there is a solution. The solution is love. The solution is faith. The solution is experiencing the Church, not as an enemy, but as the circle in which God wants to encounter all people. Let us understand this Church; let us be inspired with this love; let us live this faith, and I assure you that there will be a solution to all of our great social problems.

As archbishop, I also want to thank all you who work in harmony with the Church's lines of action, all you who enlighten others by your faith and inspire them with your love, all you who prudently teach the Church's social doctrine. Thank you, dear sisters and brothers, all you who accompany us in this hour of sorrow.

The One Mass

(March 20, 1977)

Over the next week, Romero reflected on how the Church should respond to the rising persecution and violence. On the very day of the funeral Mass for Rutilio Grande, Manuel Solórzano, and Nelson Lemus, he wrote to the country's president, saying that he would no longer participate as archbishop in any official government events until the government "put all its efforts into making justice manifest in regard to this unprecedented sacrilege." No serious official governmental investigation into the deaths of Grande, Solórzano, and Lemus (and many others) ever took place. Although Romero maintained an open line of dialogue and communication with government officials, over the next three years he refused to attend presidential inaugurations and other formal events. In a country where the ecclesiastical and civic leaders were traditionally united, such refusal was a bold step of protest and a declaration of the freedom of the Church from the political authorities. But this was just the beginning of Romero's week.

The bishops of the country gathered the next day, on March 15, as did the clergy of the archdiocese. Romero consulted extensively with both groups, but also felt his responsibility as archbishop to lead his people. That evening a news bulletin went out from the archdiocese under the name of the archbishop. It announced the Church's refusal to participate in official government events, suspended classes at all Catholic schools for three days of reflection, and announced that the only Mass to be celebrated in the entire archdiocese the following Sunday would be at 10:00 a.m. at the cathedral. That Mass came to be known as *la misa única,* "the One Mass."

Romero did not make these decisions lightly, and he did so in consultation with his clergy. However, not all were pleased. The papal nuncio, who maintained close relationships with government officials and business leaders, summoned Romero to his office. He rebuked the archbishop and tried to convince him to reverse the decision on the One Mass in particular. Some of Romero's fellow bishops, though still publicly united, expressed their concerns and displeasure behind the scenes. In response, Romero again summoned the clergy of the diocese to vote on the matter behind the scenes. They voted nearly unanimously to implement the announced plan. That Sunday, Romero presided over the one and only Mass in the archdiocese, with over one hundred thousand people in attendance. For Romero, the One Mass was a clear, prophetic statement: the Church, as one, would affirm the witness of Rutilio Grande and walk united along the path of the Gospel.

Romero carefully prepared his homily for that Sunday. What was the purpose of the One Mass? Why the unprecedented decision to gather everyone together at the cathedral? And how could he counter those who would misconstrue the event as a political gathering? People typically quote one line from Romero's March 20 homily. It is a truly powerful moment and one that he himself will repeat again later: "Beloved priests, let us remain united in the authentic truth of the Gospel. This is another way for me to say, as Christ's humble successor and representative here in the archdiocese, that *anyone who attacks one of my priests, attacks me.*" The One Mass was a sign of unity and solidarity within the archdiocese. That day, Romero keenly felt the presence and support of the people and his clergy gathered around him, and they received his uncompromising commitment to them.

Three other themes stand out from the homily in light of the historical moment and Romero's wider homiletic corpus. First, his homily offers an accessible catechesis on the significance of the Mass and the sacraments. Such catechesis is typical of his preaching and reflects his self-understanding of his teaching role as bishop. Early in the homily, he encourages the massive crowd to recognize that the Mass is Christ. Then, a minute later, he sharpens this basic point: "The Mass is Christ *who evangelizes.*" "Evangelization" and related words arise frequently in Romero's homilies. The word comes from the Greek *evangelion,* meaning "Good News," and is sometimes translated as "Gospel." Thus, the first line of the Gospel of Mark reads, "The beginning of the good news (*evangelion*) of Jesus Christ." And St. Paul declares, "I am not ashamed of the Gospel (*evangelion*)" Rom 1:16). The Christian life is one of evangelization, of being sent forth to proclaim the good news of the Gospel in word and deed. But, for each of us, responding to this call is the journey of a whole life. Romero compares each of us to the prodigal son who anxiously seeks happiness in all the wrong places. The Mass then offers a healing and reorienting encounter. Here one does not encounter "God" in a generic sense, but rather the concrete, evangelizing presence of Jesus Christ who heals, forgives, sanctifies, and calls.

Second, Romero emphasizes that this encounter sends forth the whole community to live out that good news. Evangelization is the mission of the Church. But this only begs further questions: What are the basic contours of "evangelization?" What does an authentic living out of the good news look like? As we have already seen, in his homily a week earlier, he named "the inspiration of faith," "the social doctrine of the Church," and "the motivation of love" as three defining features of true Christian engagement with the world. In his homily for the One Mass, he reflects on maintaining a "healthy balance" in our understanding of evangelization. Here Romero argues for a middle way between two extremes. On the one hand, true evangelization does not remain up in the clouds, unconcerned with the reality of the world around it. Think about how many Christians fail to see the work of social justice as a truly Christian work. For Romero, such failure demonstrates a fundamental misunderstanding of the Gospel, a myopic vision unwilling to see the Gospel in its fullness. However, Romero also warns that one must always be on guard against the temptation to reduce the Gospel to nothing but the quest for social justice. In this case, the Gospel will almost inevitably be transformed into a secular political program and the language of the Gospel will be manipulated to "justify doctrines that are not those of Christ." He will seek to explore this "healthy balance" in many homilies to come.

Finally, Romero returns to the heart of the Mass: the encounter with Christ who evangelizes. Catholic theology emphasizes that Christ is present in the Mass in a fourfold way: in the Eucharist, the word, the priest, and the people. Romero's homily focuses on the first two and the twofold encounter they invite: an encounter with Christ in the proclamation of the word and an encounter with Christ in the Eucharist. As we will see in many homilies to come, Romero had a profound confidence in the word of God and its power to speak into our lives and social worlds—if only we would listen. That same word is encountered at the table. And, as he beautifully concludes, this encounter is offered at every Mass, "whether it is celebrated by the pope in the Vatican, by the bishop in his cathedral, or by the humble pastor in the humblest village of the diocese."

Suggestions for Further Reading

Many of the homilies in the remainder of this book will explore the theme of evangelization. For those with an interest in further reading on the Eucharist, two of Romero's homilies on the feast of Corpus Christi offer rich explorations of the Mass and the sacrament.

- "Christ, the Living Bread that Gives Life to the World" (May 28, 1978) in *A Prophetic Bishop Speaks to His People: The Complete Homilies of Archbishop Óscar Arnulfo Romero*, 6 vols., trans. Joseph Owens, SJ (Convivium Press, 2015–2016), 2.467–81.

- "The Eucharist is the Living and Life-giving Presence of Christ in History" (June 17, 1979) in *A Prophetic Bishop Speaks*, 4.485–500.

Sunday, March 20, 1977
Mass Readings
Joshua 5:9a, 10–12; 2 Corinthians 5:17–21
Luke 15:1–3, 11–32

My dear sisters and brothers.

Welcome to this ancestral home of the diocese. As the lowliest member of the whole Church family, but chosen by God to be the sign of unity, this bishop thanks you warmly for joining him in giving the awaiting world the Church's word. This word of the Church not only comes from our lips but is proclaimed by our presence here at the only Mass that is celebrated in the archdiocese today.

Through this celebration we want to give great value to the Masses that are celebrated in all our parishes, in all our chapels—the value that the Mass has when a family in mourning asks that it be celebrated for a relative who is about to be buried or when a family gathers to give thanks to God on the fifteenth birthday of a daughter or to bless the marriage of two people who promise to love one another until death. At this time the Mass is recovering all its value. Perhaps because it is celebrated so frequently, it is often seen as an adornment and does not possess the greatness that it is reaching at this moment.

I believe that you who are participating here in this single Sunday Mass will truly feel what the Mass really is. You are welcome, sisters and brothers, and I also welcome those who have no faith in the Mass but are still present here. We know that there are many people here who do not believe in the

Mass, but they are seeking something that the Church is offering. And the Church is happy to be able to offer that which people are seeking, even though they don't realize that they have it close at hand, in every Mass that is celebrated. In every Mass that is celebrated there are two banquets, the banquet of the word that evangelizes and the banquet of the Eucharist, the Bread of Life that nourishes humankind. This is what we are doing now as a pilgrim Church, dressed in violet, in repentance, journeying toward Easter, toward the Christ who is risen because he died for us. The Mass is Christ. You who do not believe in the Mass, hear this once and for all: what you have found today is Christ.

The Mass Is Christ Who Evangelizes and Gives His Body and Blood for the Life of the World

I want to compare this great gathering to today's first reading. The people who had been delivered from slavery in Egypt arrived in the Promised Land and celebrated the Passover. That is what the Mass is: an encounter with the Promised Land, a breath of hope, or better still, the prodigal son in the gospel that was just read. The prodigal son is each one of us; he is the people; he is the one who often goes astray in search of false freedoms. He is the one searching for happiness—because God has created us for happiness—but not finding it, he leaves his father's house like a foolish child and seeks it in the world, living in luxury, vanity, disorder, and debauchery. And in the end he finds only emptiness. What a great image of someone who seeks happiness apart from God! The only work he can find is that of caring for pigs (Luke 15:15). There are so many people like that, caring for pigs, worshiping false idols, unable to satisfy their hearts with the things of this world.

I hope that this Mass, in which we have heard the Lenten gospel of the Prodigal Son proclaimed, sets many people thinking. Perhaps they come to this single Mass attracted by a sense of calling: "We do not find happiness in the world. Let us go and see if in this Mass, in this Church, we are offered something that truly responds to our longing for happiness." We say to you, sisters and brothers, if you have faith, you will find the answer here. The Mass is Christ who evangelizes. The Mass is Christ who offers his Body and Blood for the life of the world. These two realities are the Mass. At this moment we are in the first part of the Mass, the word of God; only in this word is to be found the solution to all our problems: political, economic, and social. These problems cannot be solved with human ideologies or worldly utopias or narrow Marxisms or atheisms that exclude the one force that can save: Jesus, who speaks to us of true liberation.

The Healthy Balance of Evangelization

With gratitude I remind you of the words of Paul VI when he spoke two years ago to the bishops of Latin America as they gathered in Rome: "My dear brother bishops of Latin America, you have sought earnestly for the right language to evangelize this admirable continent, this continent so full of hope. The Gospel of Christ is the answer."[1] The pope spoke about how the bishops are restlessly seeking adequate language for communicating Jesus's message and about how the Gospel is taking on new dimensions which are radiations that illuminate

---

1. Paul VI, Homily in the Mass concelebrated with the members of the Fifteenth General Assembly of the Conference of Latin American Bishops (CELAM [Latin American and Caribbean Bishops' Council]) November 3, 1974, in *L'Osservatore Romano* (November 10, 1974).

human activity on earth. The pope said, "Do not desist from that desire to evangelize the men and women of today with all of their concerns. Do not be held back by those who are insensitive to the world's problems, and do not lend yourself to the tactics of those who want to introduce into the Gospel of Christ solutions that are not Christian." Here in the pope's words we find the healthy balance of evangelization. Let no one hold us back in this language that the Church speaks; let no one tell people that there is no hope in the Church. But also, let no one abuse our language and attempt to use the Gospel to justify doctrines that are not those of Christ.

We are experiencing this balance right now, dear sisters and brothers, and so I want to thank all of these beloved priests publicly, before the whole archdiocese, as we gather here in unity around the one and only Gospel. Many of them risk danger and even the greatest sacrifice, the one which Father Grande made. Thank you. That applause ratifies the profound joy that I feel in my heart as I take possession of this archdiocese. I feel that my own weaknesses and my own inabilities find their complement, their power, and their courage in this united priesthood. Beloved priests, let us remain united in the authentic truth of the Gospel. This is another way for me to say, as Christ's humble successor and representative here in the archdiocese, that anyone who attacks one of my priests, attacks me.

Be assured, my sisters and brothers, that the evangelical line that the archdiocese follows is authentic. All those religious and lay people who collaborate with our beloved priests are secure in their positions as long as they remain in communion with their bishop. Indeed, this is the meaning of today's celebration. It is an authorization of the bishop as authentic teacher of the faith, who assures all those who are in communion with him that they are preaching a doctrine that is in communion with the pope and is therefore also the true doctrine of our Lord Jesus Christ.

Evangelization Is Incomplete without the Sacraments

My dear brothers and sisters, the reasons for following the true orientations of the pope, the Vicar of Christ, are explained to us in his latest document, which is a Magna Carta of evangelization.[2] The document states that the process of evangelization remains incomplete without the sacraments, just as this Mass would be incomplete if it ended with the word and no Eucharist. Evangelization is complete only when the sacrament of the Church is celebrated, only when the Church is experienced as a sign of Christ's presence in obedience to the hierarchy and with the concrete signs of the sacraments (*Evangelii Nuntiandi 47*). After the word, we enter into the second part of the Mass where Christ becomes our food, where Christ becomes the host, where Christ repeats his offering of Holy Thursday evening: "Take and eat; this is my body; this is my blood, which will be shed for you" (Luke 22:19). Evangelization that consisted only of words without sacraments would not build up the true Church. Evangelization that was only Bible and words—excuse me for saying this, dear separated sisters and brothers—would leave our Catholic doctrine mutilated, as happens when the sacraments are left aside. We priests preach the word, and we give that word made life in Communion. What a precious sign we have here, as the priests gather around the altar where the hosts have been prepared to be consecrated into the Body of the Lord and then distributed to the people

---

2. As he did in the previous homily, Romero refers here to Paul VI's apostolic exhortation, *Evangelii Nuntiandi*.

as nourishment for their life. Baptism and the other sacraments, like matrimony, are signs of the Christ who sanctifies life. And this is what the Church does.

Therefore, my sisters and brothers, the priests have this power which they have received from Christ, but which they exercise in communion with the bishop. This concelebration is a beautiful sign, for it shows that the priests consider the bishop as the center of their liturgy and the center of their sacramental life. They are the channels, together with the bishop, that bring the word of Christ and the life of Christ to the people who are waiting for them.

We also want to bear witness to the people who are left without Mass today so that they understand what the persecution of a priest means. What would it be like if one day this small group of priests were taken from the people? How would people be without Mass? How would the parishes be without baptisms? My sisters and brothers, I believe everyone has understood the meaning of our celebrating just one Mass today. There is nothing of demagogy in this action. The Church is not being manipulated by some political party. She is not raising a protest in a merely human manner. She is simply stating what the Mass means, whether it is celebrated by the pope in the Vatican, by the bishop in his cathedral, or by the humble pastor in the humblest village of the diocese.

And we want to urge you all to value the Mass, dear sisters and brothers. I began by welcoming you, and now I am happy to have had the opportunity to explain to you, with simple words, the meaning of the Mass. I hope that those who did not previously believe in the Mass will now become followers of that Christ who becomes present in the Mass of every Sunday and in the Mass of every human circumstance. Thank you very much for helping us give this sign that the Church wants to give.

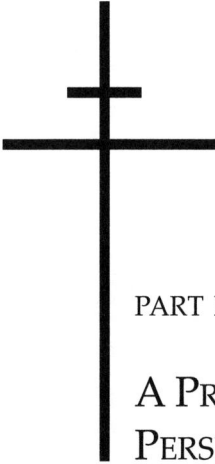

PART II

A Prophetic and Persecuted People

The Church's Mission

(May 8, 1977)

As the Salvadoran Church moved from Lent to Easter in 1977, Romero continued to grow closer to his people. Each week he saw the suffering and injustice that marked so much of Salvadoran life. In order to oppose the misinformation surrounding so many deaths and disappearances, he not only expanded the diocesan Legal Aid Office, assigning it the responsibility of receiving, documenting, and publicizing the increasing violations of human rights; he also regularly met with ordinary Salvadorans and with peaceful protestors attacked by the military. His people came to him, and he went out to them.

The people of El Salvador were coming to know their new archbishop. Not only was the cathedral packed each Sunday, Romero's preaching was also broadcast on the radio and soon became the most popular program in the country. From the capital of San Salvador to small villages in the mountains, people tuned in every week to hear Romero's homily. For them, his was a voice of truth and solidarity, the voice of someone who clearly understood their joy, hope, grief, and anxiety. From him they heard a powerful word that spoke into their lives, into their hopes, their sufferings, and the reality around them.

During the first half of 1977, that reality was increasingly marked by disunity and violence. Repressive action by the government was intensifying, but not only that: on April 19, one of the emerging guerrilla movements kidnapped the foreign minister, Maurice Borgonovo Pohl, and demanded ransom for his release. During the 1970s, these movements arose alongside the many other organizations and informal groups seeking social and political reforms. As government repression intensified in response to the clamor for change, both the popularity and violence from revolutionary groups also increased. In such a context, calls for dialogue and reconciliation were often ignored. Despite pleas from all sides, including several from Romero, Borgonovo was found dead on May 10.

The Church was likewise increasingly becoming a target of slander, misinformation, and persecution. The government expelled multiple priests from the country. The diocesan print shop was bombed. And then, the day after the body of the foreign minister was found, the White Warrior Union, a right-wing paramilitary group, killed Father Alfonso Navarro, together with a young parishioner, Luis Torres, in retaliation. For a second time—but not the last—Romero would preside at the funeral of a fallen priest. There, he urged everyone to forsake violence and slander, and instead commit to see the dignity in every life: "We say now, here before Father Navarro, the same as we said yesterday before the foreign minister Borgonovo Pohl: life is sacred, even in the humblest *campesino*, even in the priest. Even the life of a person thought to be a criminal is always sacred."

By early May, Romero himself became the target of accusations that he was leading the Church astray. The earlier supporters of his appointment as archbishop felt betrayed. They thought they were getting a shy, studious archbishop who would focus more on spiritual matters and steer clear of the social and economic struggles dominating the country. Instead, Romero increasingly became a clear and fierce defender of human dignity, wherever it was being trampled upon. As we have seen, he dramatically endorsed the witness of Rutilio Grande and removed the support the institutional Church had traditionally given to the government. Because of all this, he became the target of slanderous editorials, anonymous threats, and even formal complaints to the Vatican. He was accused of meddling in politics, supporting communism, and becoming a pawn of the left. While always admitting his own fallibility and thus a desire for dialogue, Romero drew a line in the sand: all who claimed to be Catholic had the responsibility to know and follow the teachings of the Church. The situation in El Salvador was certainly complex and confusing, but Romero insisted that the teachings of the Church are actually quite clear on certain matters if one is willing to listen. His own personal attempt to be faithful to these teachings was a hallmark of his preaching. He was clear on his commitment and blunt in his challenge to others. True theology and faithful pastoral practice will always be marked by "fidelity to the word of God and the magisterium of the Church"—a formulation he would repeat throughout his preaching in May.

When Romero speaks here of the "magisterium," he is speaking of official teachings of the Catholic Church. In light of what he saw as the fundamental errors of his critics and the needs of his time, he insisted, "We are also convinced that a priest or any Catholic would be out of communion with the Catholic faith if he or she, in the name of a tradition without evolution or immanence, that is, without involvement in real historical problems, were to reject the teaching of Vatican II, the Latin American Bishops' Conference in Medellín, the present pope [Pope Paul VI], and the diocesan bishop who is in communion with the pope." These three—Vatican II, Medellín, and Paul VI—were the foundation for his preaching and he cited each of them extensively in his homilies.

The Second Vatican Council (or Vatican II) was a universal gathering of bishops from 1962 to 1965. Your average Catholic remembers Vatican II for the reforms to Mass that it initiated. For Romero, of all the changes introduced by Vatican II, the most important was the shift in the Church's self-understanding and in its relation to the world. In his second pastoral letter (dated August 1977), he explains, "Many things in the Church have changed in recent years; for example, changes in the liturgy, in the role of the laity, in religious life, in the training given in seminaries, and so on. But the fundamental change, the change that explains all the others, is the new relationship between the Church and the world."[1] Vatican II touched upon every aspect of Catholic life, but at the heart of the Council was its vision of the pilgrim people of God journeying in the world: of each Christian called to the fullness of holiness in whatever state of life they are in; of a community called together to be a sacrament of salvation and a seed of the kingdom; and of a world meant to be consecrated to God and transformed by God's love.

Romero found this vision of the Church as *in* the world and *in service to* the world articulated particularly clearly in *Gaudium et Spes*, Vatican II's Pastoral Constitu-

---

1. Óscar Romero, *Voice of the Voiceless: The Four Pastoral Letters and Other Statements*, trans. Michael J. Walsh (Orbis Books, 1985). Translation slightly adjusted.

tion on the Church in the Modern World. The whole text speaks of the Church's solidarity with humanity and the call to bring the Gospel into every dimension of human life. Thus, without losing a clear sense of its distinctive religious mission, the Church must speak into social realities and affirm, in word and practice, the true dignity of every person. In order to carry out its mission, *Gaudium et Spes* famously asserts, "The Church has always had the duty of scrutinizing the signs of the times and of interpreting them in the light of the Gospel." The Church must always look toward the world to discern where God's grace may already be active and where sin seems to reign—and interpret how to respond to these realities in light of the word of God.

The Latin American bishops took up this exact task three years after Vatican II (in 1968) when they gathered in Medellín, Colombia. Romero refers to this gathering and the sixteen documents it produced simply as "Medellín." The texts of Medellín, among other things, receive, further develop, and apply the vision of Vatican II to the Latin American context. In particular, the texts take up the challenge of what it means to proclaim and live the Gospel in a world of social transformation, in a world marked by extreme poverty, inequality, and oppressive structures as well as by movements demanding change. The opening line of the document on justice set the foundation for thinking about the mission of the Church: "There are many studies of the Latin American people. All of these studies describe the misery that besets large masses of human beings in all of our countries. That misery, as a collective fact, expresses itself as injustice which cries to the heavens."[2] The Church

---

2. CELAM, Medellín, "Justice," par. 1. The documents of Medellín can be found in English online and in the book Second General

must not ignore such suffering. Indeed, a Church that preaches the dignity of every person is obliged to defend that dignity and promote a society worthy of the human person. In particular, the documents of Medellín continually insist on the pursuit of peace, the construction of a just society, and the empowerment of the poor and marginalized as fundamental Christian tasks, not merely political ones.

We already encountered Romero's mention of Paul VI in the previous two homilies in this book. Romero saw in Paul VI, particularly in his apostolic exhortation *Evangelii Nuntiandi* (1975), the further maturation of Vatican II and Medellín. There, the pope takes up and affirms a vision of the Church's mission as "integral," or true evangelization as "integral evangelization." "Integral" here means something like "holistic." Against both materialistic and spiritualistic reductions, *the true Gospel touches and transforms every aspect of human life.* This basic point deeply formed Romero, and he returned to it many times in his preaching. When his opponents said that he should not preach on social issues, he accused them of evading the full demands of the Gospel. He called on them to read and follow the teachings of Vatican II, Medellín, and Paul VI.

In the May 8th homily that follows, you will see Romero's response to the world around him as well as his call to fidelity to the word and the magisterium. You will also encounter one of the best syntheses of his understanding of the Church and its mission. You will see a continuation of his vision of the Church navigating the rough waters

---

Conference of Latin American Bishops, *The Church in the Present-Day Transformation of Latin America in the Light of the Council* (United States Catholic Conference, 1973).

between the extremes of spiritualistic escape and materialistic reduction. Here he appeals to the fundamental Christian idea of the incarnation—that salvation comes through the Son of God taking on our human flesh. As mentioned in the introduction to this book, this appeal is a typical moment for Romero—indeed, the verb "to incarnate" and its many variations occur over three hundred times in his homilies. He repeatedly insists that the call to enflesh the Gospel in one's life and in the world, to bring the transformative power of the Gospel into history, is what defines the Christian life. Thus, in an earlier homily focusing on God's word, he reminds us,

> [The Bible] is a divine but also human word, because it comes from God while also having human roots and having applications to the concrete realities of the earth. To be "disincarnate" and not consider earthly concerns would not be the word of God; neither would it be the word if it were incarnated in a way that we forget that it is of God, that it is the *word of God* (April 7, 1977).

On May 8 he continues this theme when he insists that the Church does not preach a "disincarnated" spirituality or love.

In his homily, Romero also takes up the thorny topic of the relationship between the Church and politics. He had already touched upon this in previous homilies and would continue to do so—particularly in light of the accusation that his preaching was meddling in politics. In this moment, he insists that the Church must never act as a political party, and that he as archbishop has no special expertise in matters of politics, economics, or law. These are frequent points in his preaching. And here, as elsewhere, he continues by insisting that the Church has the obligation to speak *a word of orientation*. The Church offers a vision of human flourishing that can guide and support all in their construction of a just society. It doesn't seek conflict with political authorities. However, as he asserts so powerfully in the homily, echoing Pope Pius XI: "The Church is not involved in politics, but when politics touches the altar, the Church defends the altar. The rights of the human person are of great concern to the Church. Whenever life is endangered, Mother Church is concerned." This too is part of the mission of the Church.

Suggestions for Further Reading

Many homilies further develop the central themes of the one that follows. Indeed, on October 9, 1977, Romero says he is getting bored of having to repeat himself so much in the face of the accusation of being a communist! Among many others, I would recommend two homilies from his first year as archbishop that richly extend his vision of the Church's mission.

- "Characteristics of Our Church" (August 21, 1977) in *A Prophetic Bishop Speaks to His People: The Complete Homilies of Archbishop Óscar Arnulfo Romero*, 6 vols., trans. Joseph Owens, SJ (Convivium Press, 2015–2016), 1.261–71.

- "The Church of Integral Development" (October 9, 1977) in *A Prophetic Bishop Speaks*, 1.354–68.

Sunday, May 8, 1977
Mass Readings
Acts 14:20b–26; Revelation 21:1–5a
John 13:31–33a, 34–35

Dear sisters and brothers and esteemed radio audience.

For the archdiocese this is a family hour. Because of this marvel of the radio we all feel like one great family, and not only those who at this moment are sheltered beneath the roof of this cathedral, symbol of the Church's unity and truth in the world. The cathedral is a special place. It is the seat of the pastor who is responsible for the unity of the whole diocese and responsible also for the truth that is preached in the diocese. Through the radio, however, we feel that the cathedral has expanded to every corner of the diocese, and we are delighted that this message is multiplied through the use of the radio.

When we speak of the radio as a "miracle", we are echoing the voice of the Second Vatican Council, which dedicated one of its documents to the means of communication such as radio, television, and the press. This document seeks to awaken Catholics to their responsibility to support the Church's own means of communication.[1] Each year one day is set aside to promote people's awareness about the importance of the media; this year it will be Sunday, May 22, two

---

1. Second Vatican Council, Decree *Inter Mirifica* on the Means of Social Communication (December 4, 1963).

weeks from now. But today I want to anticipate that event be-cause, as you all know, the Church's means of communica-tion, namely, our radio station YSAX and our newspaper *Orientación*, are the objects these days of intense persecu-tion. This week, as you know, a bomb exploded and de-stroyed some of the machinery in our printing office, Imprenta Criterio. This week we also received threats that this radio station might be closed down. Who knows whether this is the last time that you will hear me on the radio? May God will otherwise.

God wants it to be understood that the mission of the Church does not involve backing defamatory campaigns against the Church. Let it be understood that a voice is needed to speak out against those slanderous campaigns that are raging like a storm against the Church. It is not right that the Church should be silent when she must speak to de-fend herself and offer guidance to the faithful at this time of confusion. I am most happy to have received some corre-spondence on this matter. The community of Ciudad Arce sent a beautiful letter that states, "We are strengthened when we listen to your messages that are filled with opti-mism and at the same time speak the truth. In our communi-ties we pray that God will continue to strengthen you in this same spirit." Thank you very much, my beloved Christians. I know that this voice that speaks is not an isolated voice, for when a representative individual speaks, the whole or-ganism expresses itself through that mouth. So also, the mys-tical Body of Christ is an organism in which every last Christian takes part, including the persecuted, the silenced, and the tortured Christians.

The Mission of the Church

But there must be a voice that speaks for the whole organism that suffers, a voice that cries out and speaks the truth, a voice that encourages and strengthens. I honestly feel, sisters and brothers, that I am that voice and that we are fulfilling a mission. That is precisely what we stated in the message that you all probably read in the papers this week.[2] On the one hand, we are in solidarity with the anguish and the hope of the people of our time, especially those who are poor and who suffer. On the other hand, be aware that we are not being political when we speak in this way. The Council has stated (and I put these words in quotation marks): "The Church has the right to pass moral judgments, even on matters touching the political order, whenever basic personal rights or the salvation of souls make such judgments necessary" (*Gaudium et Spes* 76). When I was a student in Rome, I was deeply moved by a very beautiful statement of Pope Pius XI: "The Church is not involved in politics, but when politics touches the altar, the Church defends the altar." The rights of the human person are of great concern to the Church. Whenever life is endangered, Mother Church is concerned. At this moment the Church is very mindful of the many mothers who are suffering in our land. The Church is concerned about those who are unable to speak, those who suffer, and those who are tortured or silenced. This is not being political. Rather, those involved in politics are touching

---

2. "Declaration of the Archbishop and Clergy of the Archdiocese of San Salvador on Recent Events," in *Orientación* (May 8, 1977). Unless indicated otherwise, quoted passages in this homily are from this message.

the altar and touching morality, and the Church has the right to speak its word of moral orientation.

It will be said that this is Marxism. I am not going to read right now the whole message that was published this week because it is too long; at the end of the Mass that message will be read here over the radio. But I want you to pay heed to the part of the message where it says, "We want to remind you that we are human and therefore have limitations and can be mistaken." I fully recognize, sisters and brothers, that I am a man and I can make mistakes. That is why I am open to dialogue. Anyone who is not in agreement with me, come and let us talk with one another. Convince me of my errors. But don't criticize me or silence me without first listening to me. We are aware of our limitations and we know that we can be mistaken. As human persons we can all make mistakes. Nevertheless, the message speaks for all the priests united with the archbishop when it states, "We want to be faithful to our prophetic mission in order to guide the people in the midst of such great confusion." This is our intention; do not distort it. We want to guide and give witness to the people of God who listen to us and read our bulletins; they are seeking orientation. Let us not silence this voice that offers guidance. Let us correct the possible errors. We are willing to dialogue and to let them tell us how we are abusive or in what we are mistaken. These are accidental matters that can be corrected. But let us speak, and let us offer guidance. "Therefore we restate our oath of fidelity to the word of God and the magisterium of the Church." This is the guidance that the priest offers: the word of God and the Church's magisterium.

In the light of God's word and the Church's magisterium, we must speak in the same way that Peter addressed the authorities in Jerusalem when he said, "We must obey God rather than men" (Acts 5:29). And we must also obey the magisterium of the Church. "Therefore we are conscious"— note the balance we propose here—"that we would not be in communion with our Church if we proclaimed and worked for a liberation that was merely political or socio-economic." In other words, if the liberation and redemption that the Church preaches through her priests seek only a political or economic sort of redemption—after the fashion of Marxism, which has no faith in God or hope in heaven—then it would not be the true message of the Church. Let it be very clear, then, that when the Church preaches social justice, equality, and human dignity; when the Church defends those who suffer poverty or violence, this is not subversive nor is it Marxism. This is the authentic magisterium of the Church. I sincerely hope, dear sisters and brothers, that we are all interested in knowing what the Church has been saying since the Second Vatican Council.

This does not mean breaking with traditions of twenty centuries; rather, the Church is adapting the tradition to these modern times. And you can see that it is easy to confuse our message with Marxism if one is not aware that the Church lives by hope, by God, by spirituality, by prayer. This gives the Church an even greater impulse to work for liberation of the earth than the communists have, for she knows that no paradise such as the communists announce exists in this world. Paradise is consummated there in eternity, but the kingdom of God is already happening here on earth, as the Book of Revelation told us today (Revelation 21:1). Christ came to establish with his resurrection a new human situation of holiness and justice and love. It is not necessary to wait until we die in order to possess heaven. Already on earth love is proclaimed. And as long as there is no love, we will have only that sad reality of people preying like wolves on one another.

This is what happens when Christ's love is extinguished in our hearts. Yet it is precisely love that the Church preaches, love even for those who persecute and calumniate her. As Christ said, "Love your enemies and pray for those who persecute you" (Luke 6:27). "Do good to those who hate you" (Matt 5:44). This is what we preach: No to vengeance! No to the class struggle! No to violence! You would have to be blind to believe that, in these circumstances of violence and persecution, we have not sided with those who suffer, whether they be poor or rich. We have defended the life of the foreign minister, Borgonovo Pohl,[3] and we will continue to defend it. We do not want them to make him a victim of violence. But along with Borgonovo Pohl's mother who is suffering, we are in solidarity also with the mothers of all those who are imprisoned, with all those who suffer. We are not on the side of one particular class of people.

I also want this to be very clear, sisters and brothers, because some people have said that the new archbishop does not want to be the bishop of the rich, but only of the poor. This is a lie. That phrase is part of the defamatory campaign. From the beginning everyone has heard me say: I am with everyone. I am open to dialogue with everyone. I am willing to correct my mistakes. And I will speak with anyone from any sector. I love everyone, and my mission is to love people in order to save them. In my heart there is no room for exclu-

---

3. On April 19, 1977, the FPL (Popular Forces of Liberation) kidnapped Mauricio Alfredo Borgonovo, government foreign minister, to obtain the freedom of thirty-seven political prisoners. The minister's family requested the mediation of Archbishop Romero, who accepted the request and promised to do all he could to save Borgonovo's life. See "Statement of the Archbishop of San Salvador on the Borgonovo Pohl Case" (April 26, 1977) in *Orientación* (May 1, 1977): 3.

sion, sisters and brothers, and I say this to you in total frankness. Therefore, the mission of the Church should not be confused with Marxism or subversion or hatred, for this would be a betrayal of the Church's mission. If any priest is convinced of subversion or Marxism, then we must separate that individual from the Church—but he must be convinced of that in judgment and in truth.

On the other hand, notice how balanced the Church is when she denies being subversive or Marxist. Our declaration continues: "We are aware that we would not be in communion with our Church if we announced a liberation that was merely political or socio-economic. But we are also convinced that a priest or any Catholic would be out of communion with the Catholic faith if he or she, in the name of a tradition without evolution or immanence, that is, without involvement in real historical problems, were to reject the teaching of Vatican II, the Latin American Bishops' Conference in Medellín, the present pope, and the diocesan bishop who is in communion with the pope. For it is the bishop, in communion with the pope, who is the only teacher authorized to teach and endorse the authentic teaching of the Church in his diocese."

Yes, sisters and brothers, for while one side accuses the Church of being Marxist and subversive, another group of people wants to submit the Church to a tradition without immanence, that is, a disembodied [*desencarnada*] spirituality, a Protestant-style preaching that floats in the clouds, that sings psalms and prays, but without any concern for temporal realities. These people are not Catholic either, because all the modern documents of the Church are inspired precisely in the words of today's gospel reading: "This is how all will know that you are my disciples, if you have love for one another" (John 13:35). The modern preaching of the Church emphasizes this fraternal love. Perhaps we previously placed too much emphasis on loving God, and we thought we were loving God while we were treating our sisters or brothers badly. Today the Church demands of us: if you truly love God, then do good to your neighbor, your worker, your subordinate, and the prisoner. Then we would find love even in our prisons, and there would no longer be that hatred and that violence that is so prevalent in our time.

The Church, then, keeps this careful balance and wants those Catholics who do not understand this modern teaching of the Church to learn about it. (Sadly, one priest who is not in communion with the Church has written recently against this teaching.[4]) The Church does not preach a spiritualized [*desencarnado*] love of God but rather a love of God that is revealed in the love of neighbor. I recommend that you reflect seriously on this message because it contains nothing that is subversive; it is simply a message of orientation.

Finally, dear sisters and brothers, we want to say that the Church cannot remain silent. She must speak out, and if unfortunately they also want to silence this radio station, then look for the word of God from the priest in your parish. Do not miss Mass on Sunday. The diocesan office will take care to continue publishing its informational bulletin. Look for it in your parishes. Do not become isolated from this communion of the word, for the persecuting forces who defame the Church have at their disposition all the newspapers and all radio and television stations, thus creating an unequal struggle. But the Church is not looking for a fight; she simply wants to state what she represents. Therefore let us get to know her well. Even if you want to condemn her, we must first know her

---

4. The reference is to Father Ricardo Fuentes Castellanos, who frequently wrote against the archbishop, the archdiocese, and the teachings of the Church coming out of Vatican II.

before doing so. Do not condemn the Church, especially her children, without hearing her first, without listening to her message, without carefully discerning the news about her that is so often distorted. Please then, dear sisters and brothers, let us remain in the communion of the word. The Church is launching a campaign to help our own means of communication. Along with the letter from Ciudad Arce, we received the first contribution of thirty-nine *colones* collected from the poor. They are a sign of hope and tell us that the Church is not alone. I have also received early contributions from a priest and another *campesino*. You can make your own contribution through your pastor or by bringing it to the chancery. Let us do our part to maintain the Church's means of communication.

Prayer Is Primary

In the second place, I want to ask you, dear sisters and brothers, to pray often. Not that prayer is secondary; rather, it is primary, and second only in the order in which I am expressing my ideas. This is the month of May, the month of the Virgin, the month of much prayer. The Catholic schools met this past week in a gesture of solidarity, and they are aware that a terrible campaign is being waged against them. We know that this campaign is aimed at the destruction of the Catholic schools. We also know that something called "The National Commission for the Defense of the Catholic Doctrine" is planning to establish its own school. We just stated that the bishop alone is authorized to endorse the Catholic teaching of the diocese. No one else should presume to exercise vigilance over Christian doctrine in the schools. In the light of this situation, it was suggested that we need to pray, and it was decided that May 13, the feast of Our Lady of Fatima, will be set aside as a day of prayer. I support this initiative of the schools because I want this to be a day of prayer not only for the schools but for the whole diocese.

On May 13 at 10:00 in the morning we will celebrate a solemn Mass in the cathedral with representatives from the schools, and I also invite the parishes to send representatives. On the same day, as you know, in the scenic mountains of Las Pavas in Cojutepeque, prayers will be offered to the Virgin of Fatima. Also, in La Rábida and in Los Planes de Renderos, places consecrated to the Virgin of Fatima, the parish churches will be special centers of prayer. I ask all the parishes and the priests to organize a Holy Hour on this feast of Our Lady of Fatima, so that all the people on that day can earnestly ask the Virgin to intercede on our behalf. Let us pray earnestly for our country and for our archdiocese. Let us there-fore celebrate this Holy Hour in all the parishes on May 13, but let us not be satisfied to pray on just that one day. I ask of you all during the month of the Virgin: let us give new life to the beautiful traditions of our people, with processions through the streets of our villages and with flowers from the fields. The flowers that fill the church and surround the image of the Virgin are signs of the prayers of our people. In the schools and in the seminary they are celebrating this month of May with great devotion. With regard to this program of prayer, sisters and brothers, I want to remind you that every day in the cathedral there is exposition of the Blessed Sacra-ment. So when you come from the towns and villages and pass near the cathedral, come in and pay a visit to the Blessed Sacrament; pray for the needs of the Church, and the country.

Solidarity with the Jesuits

Another thought, sisters and brothers, regarding our com-munion as a family, is the solidarity of the archdiocese with the Society of Jesus, that is, the Jesuits. We can speak of them in the same way that we speak of other priests: they can make mistakes. Nevertheless, regarding the substance of what they teach, I ask you to study the history of the Society of Jesus since it was founded in the sixteenth century by Saint Ignatius Loyola in response to the dangers of that time, very similar to those of today. The Jesuits came to form a valiant army of men who were always at the vanguard of the Church. That is why they are called "the company," a military term of those days that referred to those at greatest risk during battle. So it is natural that the Jesuits are always the targets when the Church is attacked.

But take note: the Company of Jesus, the Jesuits, is not some sect separated from the Catholic Church; they are part of the Catholic Church. Anyone who attacks a Jesuit attacks the Church. That is why we are saddened. This coming week, if we are allowed to do so, a paid ad will be published with the title, "The Jesuits and the Capture, Detention, and Deportation of Father Jorge Sarsanedas."[5] I myself went to the barracks of the National Guard to receive Father Sarsanedas and take him from there to the airport to get a flight to Panama, where he is now. I want to make it clear that I could not sign the release document because it contained many false statements, which I made known there.[6] But I state clearly that I am in complete solidarity as pastor of the Church with the Society of Jesus,

---

5. *La Prensa Gráfica* (May 10, 1977).

6. The National Guard arrested Father Jorge Sarsanedas, a Panamanian Jesuit, on May 1, 1977 when he was returning from celebrating Mass in Tutultepeque (Nejapa). On May 6 he was expelled from the country after having been tortured. See "Declaration of the Archbishop and Clergy of the Archdiocese of San Salvador on Recent Events" in *Orientación* (May 8, 1977).

which has always been for our Church a strong, powerful, and valiant bastion.

I am thankful because our archdiocese has already been bathed in the blood of one Jesuit, Father Rutilio Grande. Now another Jesuit has been deported, and we do not know what will happen next. We pray to God and to the Virgin for understanding. We pray that the Church's message will be understood. We cannot continue to scour the countryside and deport people. Rather, we must understand what is happening in order to take advantage of the goodness that is in each person. We must assume, dear sisters and brothers, an attitude of dialogue and understanding. Even our enemy has an aspect of goodness and good will.

A Greeting to Mothers

I want to conclude by heartily congratulating mothers. As we said at the beginning of this Mass: you mothers who suffer like Mary at the foot of the cross know that you are not alone. The Church is with you, not in some subversive way or with devious intentions, but through love, as you heard in today's message of the word of God. Love is the sign that Christ left us. And I want to tell all of you, sisters and brothers, both those listening by radio and those present in the cathedral: even if they close down all our means of communication, there will still remain a great microphone in the world—the Christian mother, the Christian community. Of course, it is true that in the time of Saint Paul and Barnabas, as we heard in the first reading, there were no radios or newspapers. But it is said that if Saint Paul were to live today, he would be a journalist. Yet Paul, even though he had no radio or newspaper, traveled about establishing Christian communities, and these communities spoke out.

Mothers are like the sacrament of God's love. The Arabs say that God, whom we cannot see, created mothers, whom we can see, and that in mothers we see God, we see love, we see tenderness. Would that all mothers would embrace this love that the Church preaches! Would that they knew how to tell others, "No, this is not subversion, this is not politics, this is not hatred. It is love like that which we have for our children." If they did this, how great would be the influence of mothers and wives on politicians, government officials, capitalists, and businessmen! Human relations would be humanized if mothers had more influence on the hearts of those who hold the reins of history. Remember that famous Roman mother: when Rome was about to be destroyed by a traitor, the Senate sent the mother of that traitor to her son to try to convince him, and Rome was saved, thanks to this mother.

Mothers, this is the role you have at this time: saving our land. Therefore the Church understands you and loves you and stands by you, just as you stand by the Church. If some of you, because of this defamation, doubt the universal love of the Church, then I ask you a question. Would you be happy if we doubted the love you have for your children simply because some enemy of yours defamed you and said, "This woman does not love her children. She hates them and persecutes them"? Yes, it would be a horrendous defamation to misrepresent a mother's love. Well, understand that the Church is a mother. The Church as a mother understands the mothers of children and says to them, "Let us keep solidarity, women, because I also am Church, I am woman, I am mother, and I love and defend the truth my Divine Spouse entrusted to me for my children. Help me."

When the Second Vatican Council was ending, the Council fathers presented the final documents to a woman who represented all the mothers of the world. You can read that beautiful message of the Council to women. It says in part, "You women have always had ... an understanding of cradles. You are present in the mystery of a life beginning. You know how to make truth sweet, tender, and accessible, as hard as it may be. Receive this teaching and pass it on to your sons and your daughters."[7] Christian mothers, how the face of El Salvador would be transformed—at this time of violence, bloodshed, suspicion, and misunderstanding—if mothers who have the mission of loving and uniting their children could unite all of us Salvadorans!

We are going to offer this Eucharist for these intentions, praying in a special way for all mothers. My sisters and brothers, if I have been mistaken in anything that I have said here, it is because I am human. I will always recognize my error if someone comes to dialogue with me and convinces me. But if I have spoken the truth, even though it hurts, let us accept it because only "the truth will set you free" (John 8:32), as Jesus said.

---

7. Second Vatican Council, Messages of the Council to the World, address by Pope Paul VI (December 8, 1965), "To Women," 5, 10.

A Torch Raised High

(June 19, 1977)

"*Sentir con la Iglesia*" — "To feel and think with the Church." Romero adopted this traditional Jesuit phrase as his episcopal motto, and it offers a helpful distillation of his vision as bishop. Romero had an unwavering commitment to the Church. We have already seen his frequent appeals to Church documents and teachings. Rare is a homily in which he doesn't cite Vatican II, Medellín, or Paul VI. In part, this emphasis was defensive. Accused of having departed from Church teaching, Romero certainly felt the need to demonstrate his fidelity. But he also simply loved and trusted the teachings of the Church; he saw them as a sure guide to living the Christian life in the world. He studied these texts carefully and required his clergy to do the same.

However, just as Romero himself grew and changed over the course of the 1970s, so did his understanding of his call as a bishop. *Sentir con la Iglesia* flourished into a deep, *two-fold* commitment. *Sentir con la Iglesia* came to mean to feel and to think with the People of God and particularly with the poor and those who suffer. This second dimension grew significantly during Romero's time as bishop of Santiago de María (1974–1976) and became a defining characteristic of his ministry as archbishop.

Put simply, Romero was close to his people. He knew his people. He loved his people. He taught them, but he also allowed himself to be taught by them. As he could say quite simply, "I delight to be in the midst of my people and to feel the kindness of all these folks" (September 25, 1977). He made his home a simple room among the sick and dying at a hospice center and invited others to join the community there for a holy hour of adoration the first day of each month. Romero was also intentional in how he travelled throughout his diocese each week to be with his people. He rejoiced in visiting parishes so clearly alive with the fervor of the Gospel, but he also saw firsthand the violence, injustice, and oppression that marked so much Salvadoran life.

On May 17, 1977, the suffering of Romero's people intensified when the town of Aguilares became the site of an extensive military operation. Over the course of a day, dozens of townspeople were killed, many *campesinos* were removed from their land, three Jesuit priests were arrested and quickly expelled from the country, and the soldiers occupied the parish church as a barracks. Within the church, soldiers shot open the tabernacle containing the reserved Eucharist, scattering the consecrated hosts on the floor. Romero attempted to go to Aguilares that day, but the military would not allow him to enter the town. After two long months, the military left. Romero returned to Aguilares to be with this suffering people and reconsecrate the church. His homily from June 19 captures his mission well: *Sentir con la Iglesia*.

This is also a crucial moment for our own memory of Romero. It is very easy for our memory of someone like Romero to become distorted. It is easy to imagine him above, beyond, and outside of his people, as a sort of light shining into the darkness, as a sort of solitary beacon of holiness illuminating a sinful world all around him. This temptation is even stronger now that Romero is officially *Saint* Óscar Romero. But we must resist distortion. Not only is it simply inaccurate, it is not how Romero himself would want to be remembered.

We must always remember Romero *with his people.* Indeed, he would take it as the greatest of honors to say that he joined the thousands of other faithful Salvadoran witnesses working in the vineyard of the Lord. On June 19, Romero emphasized this great cloud of witnesses. In his homily he mentions Father Rutilio Grande, of course, who had been killed three months earlier on his way to Aguilares; he likewise names the Jesuit priests recently expelled by the military; but he also emphasizes the faithfulness of many ordinary Christians. He points to hundreds of lay persons committed to carrying forth the mission of the Church. And in the most famous line from his homily that day, he lifts up the suffering people of Aguilares: "You are the image of the Divine One who has been pierced."

We should always remember Romero *with* this people; as *one* faithful witness among *many.* He made sure the people of Aguilares heard this word of solidarity: "We are truly with you, and we want you to know, sisters and brothers, that your pain is the Church's pain." And not only does Romero seek to comfort and guide his people, he lifts them up. For all of those seeking to stay on the Christian path in the midst of the darkness of history—including Romero himself—he proclaims, "Aguilares is a torch raised on high."

Yet, as we have seen him emphasize in every homily thus far, Romero urges the people of Aguilares not to give in to hatred, violence, and the desire for revenge. Here Romero calls on all to incarnate—to give flesh to—the peculiar two-fold love that should mark the Christian life: on the one hand, the passionate, merciful love of the Good Samaritan—the love that goes forth to those who suffer. And, it must be added, a love that takes sides and defends human dignity. Romero is clear here: in the midst of the torture, violence, and repression, the Church stands on the side of the suffering people of Aguilares and against their oppressors. True Christian love includes an unrelenting defense of the rights of the poor, abused, and victimized: "Truly I tell you, just as you did it to one of the least of these brothers and sisters of mine, you did it to me" (Matt 25:40). Yet, on the other hand, true Christian love has an odd way of "siding against" the oppressor. Even as such love forces one to take sides in the struggle, the Christian call to love is universal: love your enemy.

Romero on many occasions insisted that he was the bishop of all, that he was committed to both the poor and the rich. The love of Christ goes forth to all, even to those who inflicted such violence and suffering on the people. This love takes the form of a call for conversion:

> Let us certainly be firm in defending our rights, but let us do so with great love in our hearts, because by defending in this way, with love, we are also seeking the conversion of sinners. That is the revenge of Christians! Let us pray for the conversion of those who have assaulted us. Let us pray for the conversion of those who had the sacrilegious audacity to profane this holy tabernacle. Let us pray for pardon and also for the needed repentance of those who have made this place a prison and a torture chamber.

This is the same message he had at the funeral of Rutilio Grande, Manuel Solórzano, and Nelson Lemus when he addressed the murderers as "brother criminals." And what is striking with Romero is that *he actually means it*. In a world marked by violence, he challenged himself and all of us to bring together an uncompromising demand for transformative justice with a desire for real reconciliation. He names the violent oppression for the sin that it is while urgently seeking the conversion of all—both poor and rich—to the true common good. And on the path to such a world, he lifted up the people of Aguilares as "a torch raised on high."

Suggestions for Further Reading

Two homilies soon after his words in Aguilares continue Romero's message in a powerful way. Just a week later, on June 26, he explored the theme of Christian love in service to the kingdom of God; and two months later he spoke again of the people of Aguilares and their embodiment of a Gospel truly alive in the world.

- "Responsibility for God's Kingdom" (June 26, 1977) in *A Prophetic Bishop Speaks to His People: The Complete Homilies of Archbishop Óscar Arnulfo Romero*, 6 vols., trans. Joseph Owens, SJ (Convivium Press, 2015–2016), 1.168–75.

- "The Church of the Covenant and of True Poverty" (August 28, 1977) in *A Prophetic Bishop Speaks*, 1.272–82.

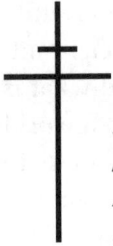

Sunday, June 19, 1977
Mass Readings
Zechariah 12:10–11; Galatians 3:26–29
Luke 9:18–24

Dear religious women, who represent this portion of God that has been consecrated in a special way for the service of the Church, and dear faithful, especially my beloved sons and daughters of Aguilares.

It is my job to gather up the assaults, the bodies, and all that the persecution of the Church leaves in its wake. Today I have come to gather up in this church and in this profaned convent a destroyed tabernacle and above all else a people that has been disgracefully humiliated and sacrificed. Therefore as I come here finally—I have wanted to be with you from the beginning, but I was not permitted to enter—I bring you, sisters and brothers, the word that Jesus commands me to share with you: a word of solidarity, a word of encouragement, a word of orientation, and finally a word of conversion.

A Word of Solidarity

In the first place, I want to express to you a cordial word of solidarity. We are with you now, and we have been with you at every moment. Indeed, if the Church can ever say, "We have been with you in a very special way", it is in these circumstances of Aguilares, because chief among their victims are three beloved priests who have been shackled and exiled.

Yet Father Carranza has said it well: "The harsh voice of rifles will be silenced, and the prophetic voice of God will continue to resound."[1] The word of God is once again here, sisters and brothers, to tell you that God always rejects violence. God has no dealings with those who kill, with those who persecute, with those who assault. That startling saying of the Lord, "All who take up the sword will perish by the sword" (Matt 26:52), promises terrible consequences if sincere conversion does not first overtake the sinner. We suffer with those who have suffered so greatly. We are truly with you, and we want you to know, sisters and brothers, that your pain is the Church's pain.

Today's first reading becomes highly expressive when the prophet bewails the desolation of Jerusalem, but at the same time he announces that the Lord's mercy and goodness will rain down upon the suffering people. You are the image of the Divine One who has been pierced, the one of whom the first reading speaks in prophetic, mysterious language. That figure representing Christ nailed on the cross and pierced by the lance is the image of all those people who, like Aguilares, have been pierced and violated. But if you suffer with faith and give your suffering redemptive meaning, then Aguilares will sing a joyful hymn of liberation because when they look on the one they have pierced they will repent, and they will see the heroism and the joy of those whom the Lord blesses in their suffering.

Therefore, sisters and brothers, our solidarity extends also to our many beloved dead and our murdered friends. In

---

1. Father Salvador Carranza, Father Marcelino Pérez, and Father José Luis Ortega were the three exiled Jesuit priests. "Father Salvador Carranza's Letter from Exile" was published in the diocesan newspaper, *Orientación*, on June 19, 1977.

this Mass we ask eternal rest for them, certain that the Lord will grant them this blessing and that from their place in heaven they will continue to work for this holy liberation that Aguilares has set in motion. We also suffer with those who are lost, with those whose whereabouts is unknown, and with those who are fleeing and don't know what is happening with their families. We are witnesses of this suffering and this separation. We experience it close at hand, because as pastors we experience the aching trust of those who through the Church hope to reunite again with those whom cruelty has dispersed. But be assured, dear sisters and brothers, that in the eyes of God they are not lost; rather, they are very close to the heart of the Lord even though their families who cannot find them are in pain. For God there is no one lost. For God there is only the mystery of suffering which, if accepted as sanctification and redemption, will also be redemptive suffering like that of Christ our Lord.

We are united with those who suffer tortures. We know that many are in their homes suffering those pains and those humiliations. May the Lord give them courage, and may they know how to forgive. Be aware, sisters and brothers, that God condemns violence, wherever it comes from, and especially when it comes from the armed forces, who instead of defending the people commit outrageous acts. God can never bless this violence. Know also that all your pain and suffering is well understood, for the Church interprets it, in accord with today's first reading, as redemptive suffering, as suffering from which will flow new sources of blessings for Aguilares.

A Word of Encouragement

My sisters and brothers, I want to add a word of encouragement and orientation. Take courage! Don't let your spirit flag!

In the Archdiocese of San Salvador, Aguilares already has a very special place, for it is here that Father Grande and his two beloved *campesinos* fell victim to the assassins' bullets. After that, the blatant persecution of priests and catechists has been without a doubt a sign of the Lord's favor. Jesus Christ told us in his Gospel that those who wish to be his disciples must deny themselves and take up their cross daily and follow him (Luke 9:23–24). He also said that those who want to keep their lives safe and secure, often by shameful intrigues such as hypocritically betraying a brother or sister in order to gain favor, are guilty of great treachery. If you want to save your life, you must lose it. You must hand it over sincerely to the Lord. And right here priests and lay people have handed their lives over to the Lord without thinking about martyrdom and suffering. They are giving witness, and we take this testimony from Aguilares in order to present it to all the parishes.

See how quickly the response has come: yesterday two lay people from every parish, a total of two hundred lay people committed to the Church, began a course that will conclude this afternoon in the seminary. Without a doubt they are following the heroic example of those who give their lives for Christ out of a desire to commit themselves to the Church. Indeed, this is the condition for being part of this lay movement; it is what is required of all who have received baptism and who have pledged to follow Christ through his cross and through his suffering. This example of Aguilares, then, is marvelous; it is the frontline of the Church; it is a commitment on the part of the Church's members to proclaim what is most dangerous in the Church's doctrine but also most necessary.

My sisters and brothers, I believe that we have mutilated the Gospel greatly. We have tried to live a Gospel that is very comfortable without handing over our lives. We accept only a Gospel of piety which makes us feel comfortable. But here in Aguilares you have started a bold movement with a more steadfast Gospel. In the recent publications of the Jesuits fathers[2] you have been able to read and understand that we are making a very serious commitment with Christ crucified, and this demands the renunciation of many pleasant things that we cannot have when we embrace the cross of our Lord.

We must therefore learn the meaning of that invitation of Christ: "If anyone wishes to come after me, he must deny himself" (Luke 9:23). Let us deny ourselves, let us forego our comforts, let us give up our personal opinions, and let us follow only the teaching of Christ, which may lead us to death, but which will also surely lead us to resurrection. All these heroes, the priests and catechists of Aguilares who have died for the name of the Lord, are without doubt participating already in the unfading glory of the resurrection.

A Word of Orientation

I also want to share with you a word of orientation. Do not confuse the liberation of Christ with false liberations that are merely temporal. As Christians formed by the Gospel, you have the right to organize and to make concrete decisions inspired by the Gospel. But be careful not to betray those evangelical, Christian, supernatural convictions by replacing them with liberations of a merely economic, political, or temporal sort. Even though Christians collaborate in the work of liberation with other ideologies, they must preserve the orig-

---

2. Romero refers here to a text published in *Estudios Centroamericanos,* "The Jesuits Address the Salvadoran People."

inal liberation that Saint Paul announces to us today, the liberation based on Christ and inseparable from Christ. Baptism incorporated me into Christ (Gal 3:26–27); in Christ I am one with God, and I cannot betray all that derives from that: being a new person. We become new persons who purify their hearts of all sin, new persons who do not speak with resentful hearts, new persons who never foment violence, hatred, or rancor. We love with the heart of Jesus even as we defend our rights with love, which is the power of our Church. We never promote hatred or class struggle, which are the false powers of other kinds of liberation that really leads to no liberation.

The Council has said that it is a form of modern atheism when people expect human struggle to achieve a future kingdom in which they will find great happiness (*Gaudium et Spes* 20). My sisters and brothers, if Christ and his Church are not taken into consideration, then this future kingdom will never be achieved. There will be nothing but tears, nothing but violence. No sound will be heard except that of machine guns and the violent outcries of those who are massacred. None of this leads to building up our society. Yet dying with faith in Christ, having worked in the light of Christ—*that* is authentic liberation.

Those who have been enlightened with the light of the Gospel and the teaching of the Church have become aware of how shameful is the treatment of many who are the image of God on earth. These people have discovered their rights, which they must defend in the light of Christ; they must continue this struggle, remaining always faithful to that illumination of faith and to the teaching of the Church. Doing this, they will not be deceived, for this will lead them to true redemption.

That is why I admire, and I want here to thank in a very special way, the Society of Jesus which illuminated these paths in Aguilares. Many perhaps did not understand them. Certainly those who persecuted them and struck repressively against the "gospel of subversion" did not understand anything. The gospel of the Jesuits is the Gospel of Jesus Christ and the Gospel of the Church, and there is no reason to confuse it with anything else. I want to thank the Jesuit fathers for having enlightened so many *campesinos* and for having organized so many communities with a Christian spirit and goodness of heart. With affection we remember Father Grande and his collaborators who knew how to instill into many hearts the light of the Gospel which should never be extinguished.

I therefore speak a word of encouragement because the light of the Lord will always illuminate these paths. New pastors will come, but the Gospel will remain the same. We ask future pastors to continue this work with the same light and courage. May they know how to guide the people along the true path of Christian liberation, as the Church today desires, especially on this Latin American continent. The brilliant documents of Medellín, which are authentic Church doctrine, should not be feared but understood; they should be put into practice because they provide light that will lead the people of Latin America to salvation.

In this sense Aguilares is a torch raised on high. We want to congratulate you in spite of the pain you feel because you are raising this torch on high. May you never let it be confused with other flames; rather, let it be the authentic light of Christ that shines in the midst of confusion and darkness.

A Word of Conversion

Finally, dear sisters and brothers, I offer a word of conversion. When Jesus Christ invites us to lose our lives in order to gain them (Luke 9:24), when he invites us to hand over our lives to him, he is calling us to conversion. When the first reading tells us how the people looked on the one they pierced (Zech 12:10) and how, repenting of their sins, they hoped to gain mercy from the pierced one, it is describing for us what our own attitude should be. I invite you to forgive, dear sisters and brothers, though I understand that it is very difficult to pardon after so many offenses. Still, this is the word of the Gospel: "Love your enemies, do good to those who hate you and persecute you; be perfect as your heavenly Father, who makes his rain fall and his sun shine on the fields of the good and the bad" (Matt 5:44–45).

Let there be no resentment in your hearts. May this Eucharist, which is a call to be reconciled with God and with our sisters and brothers, leave in our hearts the satisfaction that we are Christians so that there are no traces of hatred or rancor left in our souls. Let us certainly be firm in defending our rights, but let us do so with great love in our hearts, because by defending in this way, with love, we are also seeking the conversion of sinners. That is the revenge of Christians! Let us pray for the conversion of those who have assaulted us. Let us pray for the conversion of those who had the sacrilegious audacity to profane this holy tabernacle. Let us pray for pardon and also for the needed repentance of those who have made this place a prison and a torture chamber. May the Lord touch their hearts before the dreadful sentence is carried out: "All who take up the sword will perish by the sword" (Matt 26:52). May they truly repent and have the satisfaction of beholding the One they have pierced so that from his side a torrent of mercy and goodness may rain down and we all see ourselves as sisters and brothers.

How blessed will be that moment when this terrible tragedy disappears from El Salvador, this time when we live in fear of one another and when there are places where our sisters and brothers are suffering. May the Lord make these realities disappear from our midst with an outpouring of his mercy and goodness, with a torrent of graces to convert all our hearts. Indeed, the Creator has gifted us with a paradise, a truly beautiful nation which the Divine Savior has blessed with his own name. May it become truly a land where we all feel redeemed as sisters and brothers, just as Saint Paul has told us today, "There are no longer any differences, because we are all one in Christ our Lord" (Gal 3:28–29).

This is the final word I give you in this message, sisters and brothers. We are going to take that Word made flesh that is now made host and is given up for us in the Eucharist which will now be celebrated by us priests to whom God has given this mysterious power. We are going to change the bread and wine into the Body and Blood of the Lord. We are going to place it again in the tabernacle from which it was taken by sacrilegious hands, and we are going to restore it to the hearts of the people of Aguilares and all those who have come here to express their solidarity. Out of love for this sacred host, we want to love. We know that our hearts are small, but Jesus lends us his heart so that his one heart on the altar represents the hearts of all of us. Thus united we give glory to God, we give thanks because we are alive, we offer pardon to our enemies, and we ask forgiveness for our sins and the sins of our people. In this spirit, sisters and brothers, let us now celebrate the divine Eucharist.

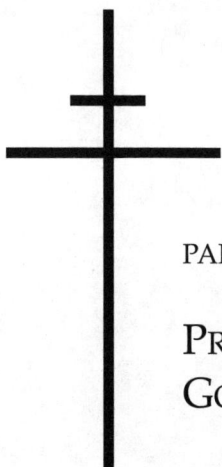

PART III

PREACHING THE GOSPEL OF CHRIST

Christ Saves All People, as a People

(Jauary 15, 1978)

Thus far in this book we have encountered four important homilies from Romero's first four months as archbishop (March–June 1977). We've seen the power of his
preaching and the way he sought to proclaim God's word
to his people. The next homily in this book is from the feast
of the Baptism of the Lord in 1978. Thematically, this homily will reinforce ideas we've come across and also introduce new ones. We'll discuss these shortly, but first, this
homily also provides the opportunity to pause and reflect
on Romero as a preacher.

By the end of 1977, Romero had settled into a standard
—yet, as we will see, quite idiosyncratic—pattern for his
homilies. They usually had a central topic (and even an explicit title) drawn from the readings of the day, three major
subsections, and then one or two additional sections reflecting on the events of the week. We'll see all these in the homily below. But we'll also see the deeper character of
Romero's preaching, the liturgical, incarnational, and catechetical quality that infused nearly every homily he gave.

If you had been listening to Romero on January 15,
1978, the first thing you would have noticed is how deeply

liturgical Romero's preaching was. He begins this homily by reminding his congregation of the journey they have all just taken from Advent, to Christmas, to the Epiphany, and now to the Baptism of Jesus. In this moment, he wants his people to remember and experience what the liturgy offers: "The heart of each of you attending Mass ought to grow in hope and joy because Christ is God, the Redeemer of humankind." This moment is typical in Romero's preaching. His homilies closely follow the rhythm of the liturgical year. Each Lent they offer some of the deepest theological accounts of what it means to journey as a people toward the cross and resurrection. His Easter homilies that follow celebrate the risen Christ and call for the Church to be a true sacrament of life. And outside of the major liturgical seasons, Romero lets himself be guided by the many feasts—both large and small—that mark the liturgical calendar. Thus, he explores the meaning of the Eucharist at each feast of Corpus Christi, Mary's role in salvation history at the feast of the Immaculate Conception, and the call to true holiness on All Saints Day. And he also pauses to reflect on popular devotions and patronal feasts that are important to the people. He often mentions an upcoming Marian procession or celebration at a particular parish. On January 15, he reflected briefly on the celebration of Christ of Esquipulas, a devotion originating in neighboring Guatemala but celebrated in El Salvador. In his preaching, Romero always invited his people to let themselves be formed by the yearly liturgical pilgrimage of the Church.

Throughout this book I have repeatedly noted Romero's insistence on the Christian life as "incarnational," as thoroughly enfleshed in the world. He critiques those "disincarnate" spiritualities that lift up prayer, devotions, and even the liturgy as a way of avoiding the call to true love of neighbor and to the building up of society. Romero equally condemned a "disincarnate" preaching, a preaching that stays up in the clouds and never touches the real challenges facing one's people and society. He explains his own approach in a simple remark on January 15: "Christ is so profoundly incarnated in our people that we celebrate him as something that is typically ours.... That is why I attempt each Sunday to present this mystery of Christ in a way that is not vague and abstract. My preaching should not be the same here in El Salvador as it would be in Africa or at some other time in history." For Romero, every homily was a chance to proclaim a *living* word into Salvadoran reality and to invite his people to be transformed by that word. As he would say later that summer in a homily focused on reading the Bible, "It's not a matter of literally repeating psalms and parables but of applying them to the concrete life of the particular time when that word of God is being preached. The Bible is like the fountain that conserves the revelation of God's word, but what use is the fountain, as crystal clear as it may be, if we don't fill our jugs from it and apply its waters to the needs of our homes" (July 16, 1978)? Romero repeats this basic idea countless times in his preaching; it expresses the incarnational commitment that shaped everything he said.

This firm conviction, along with the absence of criminal investigations, increasingly widespread repression, the breakdown of the justice system, and massive levels of disinformation flowing from media controlled by the oligarchy led Romero to regularly include one or two sections in his homilies on the happenings in the country that week. If there were two sections, one would detail the "Life of the Church," that week's events in parishes and the diocese, like confirmations, ordinations, Marian processions, feast days, and upcoming liturgical seasons; the other would focus on the "Events of the Week" in society at large. Here Romero would proclaim the truth of Salvadoran reality: of mothers longing for their kidnapped and tortured children, of rampant economic oppression, of legal justice thwarted by corruption, and of those Salvadorans demanding at least a semblance of justice. For example, in a homily from September 11, 1977:

> More sad news: tomorrow at 6:30 in the afternoon in the Sacred Heart Basilica the Cursillo Movement will celebrate the funeral of our brother, Felipe de Jesús, a great Christian and catechist. He was murdered a few days ago in El Salitre.
>
> Tomorrow also, at 11:00 o'clock in the chapel of the Rosales Hospital, I will celebrate Mass for David Agustín Cristales. His mother, who asked me to celebrate this Mass, told me, "I do not know if we should offer the Mass for the dead because he disappeared. He was a student who was going to class, and I know nothing about what happened to him. Perhaps he is already dead." I told her, "Just trust in God. We will offer a Mass and pray for his reappearance, and if he is already dead, we will pray for his eternal rest." This is a new class of dead people that has appeared in our Salvadoran society: the "disappeared."

Romero's homilies were first and foremost the proclamation of God's word. However, this proclamation also became a moment in which ordinary Salvadorans could hear the truth of what was happening to their people—of what was happening *to them.* Thus, nearly every homily of Romero's includes mentions of the violence, repression, and sin all around them. When he was critiqued for this aspect of his preaching, he returned to the principle of the incarnation: "Sisters and brothers, when I speak to you about certain events, I am not discussing things that have nothing to do with the Church. My preaching must be framed by these realities."

Finally, Romero's preaching could be described as "catechetical" in the sense of instructing the faithful in Christian belief and life. On January 15, Romero took time to give a short explanation of the purpose of Catholic education, of the liturgical seasons, of the nature of salvation, of Christ's presence in the Mass, and more. Virtually every homily he preached had a catechetical quality to it, some with long portions devoted to explaining Christian teachings and practices. He knew he had an attentive audience—in person and on the radio—and he used this time to explain the foundations of Christian life. He wasn't ashamed of doing catechesis: "I am very happy when others call [my homily] catechesis, because they don't want to call it a homily. It gives me great pleasure to feel that I am the catechist of the diocese" (April 9, 1978). "Catechist of the diocese": this names well what Romero actually did in his homilies and how he affirmed the traditional role of the bishop as teacher of the diocese. And, crucially, it places him among the thousands of lay catechists at the time who were risking their lives to share the word of God. Scores would be killed, many of them buried by Romero. Two years later he would join them among the faithful martyrs of El Salvador.

Turning to the contents of his homily from January 15, Romero announces, as he usually does, the core theme of his homily as well as the three major points he wanted to make:

> Today's readings present us with three priceless thoughts that we should absorb so that as Christians we will come to a greater understanding of the mystery of Christ as we move through this liturgical year. The first thought is that God wants to save everyone. The second is what Saint Paul writes in his letter: God wants to save us by forming a people on this earth. And the third thought is that God saves people by taking away the sins of the world.

In the homily we find the further development of many themes already encountered in this book: true Christian love, the repudiation of violence, the call to live incarnationally, and more. Extending these, Romero centers the homily on one of the most important teachings of Vatican II, a teaching that has deep roots in the long tradition of the Church: God does not will to save human beings "merely as individuals, without bond or link between one another. Rather has it pleased Him to bring them together as one people" (*Lumen Gentium*, 9). Romero's homily explores this point and reflects the Christian conviction that salvation is a deeply personal-yet-communal reality. Christianity affirms, against collectivism in all its forms, the dignity of each person, that each of us, in our unrepeatable particularity, is created, redeemed, and called by God into the fullness of life. And yet, against every form of individualism, our personal identities are formed at their most intimate level by relationships, and the fullness of life to which we are called is a communion of love. Salvation is a social reality; we are not saved merely as individuals: we are saved in order to enter into true love with God and neighbor. In his homily, Romero will draw upon Pope Paul VI's watershed encyclical, *Populorum Progressio*, to help his people see the concrete social implications of this vision.

The positive and holistic vision of a personal-social salvation forces Romero to speak of what opposes salvation: sin. Sin must never simply be ignored, as if letting a wound fester would bring about healing. The wound must be exposed and treated, even if that causes pain. The Christian, he says, is called to name sin for what it is and then seek to uproot the sins that dominate society and the human heart. This is the *prophetic* call of the Church that will be the central focus of the homilies in Part 4 of this book.

As you read Romero's homily from January 15, 1978, you will encounter his preaching at its most typical. The themes are drawn from readings of the day and also reflect the foundational vision of Christian life that pervades all his homilies. His preaching reflected his commitment (discussed in Part 2 above) to *"sentir con la Iglesia"* as he draws upon both Church teaching and the experience of his people to frame his remarks. And the homily is liturgical, incarnational, and catechetical. He wanted his people to be formed by their liturgical pilgrimage, to incarnate what they received into their own particular time and place, and to be catechized, to understand, receive, and live out the Gospel.

Suggestions for Further Reading

Romero explained his approach to preaching the word of God on many occasions. On September 11, 1977, he not only gave a concise account of his understanding of the word in the midst of the Christian life, he also guided his people through a close reading of the Prodigal Son. In July of 1978, he offered a wonderful homily on the preaching of the word as a part of the evangelizing mission of the Church.

- "The Church of True Independence, the Church of Authentic Liberation" (September 11, 1977) in *A Prophetic Bishop Speaks to His People: The Complete Homilies of Archbishop Óscar Arnulfo Romero*, 6 vols., trans. Joseph Owens, SJ (Convivium Press, 2015–2016), 1.294–304.

- "Sowing the Word of the Kingdom" (July 16, 1978) in *A Prophetic Bishop Speaks*, 3.96–112.

Sunday, January 15, 1978
Mass Readings
Isaiah 49:3, 5–6; 1 Corinthians 1:1–3
John 1:29–34

My brothers and sisters.

It is important that we understand ever more clearly what the Church's intention is as she gathers us together each Sunday. The mystery of Christ is gradually unfolded to the eyes of our faith. At the beginning of the liturgical year this mystery was proclaimed in the four Sundays and weeks of Advent. We participated in the divine preparations as God made ready his great plan to send his Son to save the world. We have been present at the moment that the scriptures call "the fullness of time" when Christ becomes incarnate in the womb of the young virgin of Nazareth and is born in Bethlehem. Even today that holy night brings joy to the world even though many fail to understand that the cause of that great joy for everyone is the great love of God who "so loved the world that he gave his only Son so that the world might be saved" (John 3:16).

Christmas is followed by Epiphany Sunday. The birth of this child in Bethlehem and his arrival into the world would have been useless unless he was revealed. That is what "epiphany" means: revelation or manifestation. The first to receive this revelation were the magi from the East, whom we remembered last Sunday. This Sunday we celebrate a new Epiphany, namely, the Baptism of Jesus. At the Jordan River, John the Baptist, inspired by God, points out Jesus as already present among us. The messianic era has begun: "Behold the Lamb of God who takes away the sin of the world" (John 1:29). There is no longer any salvation apart from Christ. This Sunday, then, we come together to celebrate that prolongation of the Epiphany. The heart of each of you attending Mass ought to grow in hope and joy because Christ is God, the Redeemer of humankind.

As we unfold the mystery of Christ in the course of the liturgical year, we celebrate certain feasts which help us do this, such as the feast days of the Virgin and the saints and various aspects of our faith. Today, for example, I want to highlight a popular devotion by which the liturgical year is made accessible to the masses of people. Today we celebrate the feast of the Lord of Esquipulas. This crucified Christ is also a type of Epiphany, revealing that Christ loved so seriously that he ended up nailed to a cross to save humankind. This mystery of the Savior Christ that we call the Lord of Esquipulas has great power of attraction for all Central America; it is a true bond of Central American unity. It shows that the Church possesses powers that human beings and politicians are unable to match. The Church keeps Central America united in one faith. This Central American Christ of Esquipulas becomes also Salvadoran. Here in our archdiocese there are at least three places that will celebrate today the patronal feast of the Holy Christ: the parish of San Bartolomé Perulapía will celebrate a solemn Eucharist at 4:00 o'clock in the afternoon; in Aguilares, under the name of the Lord of Mercies, they will have their solemn celebration at 11:00 o'clock this morning; and in Colón also the people will celebrate today the Christ of Esquipulas.

Christ is so profoundly incarnated in our people that we celebrate him as something that is typically ours. That is what

Christ wants to be: the Christ of the Epiphany, the God who became a child. At Christmastime we feel that this child belongs to every family; we all feel that he is ours. Thus this mystery of Christ that unfolds during the liturgical year is felt to be so intimately united to each of you and to me that we personally experience what Paul felt: "He loved me and offered himself up for me" (Gal 2:20). That is why I attempt each Sunday to present this mystery of Christ in a way that is not vague and abstract. My preaching should not be the same here in El Salvador as it would be in Africa or at some other time in history. Rather, I want to preach Christ who becomes incarnate here in El Salvador in 1978, the Christ who accompanies us through the changes of our actual history, the Christ who sheds light on the events of this week. This is the Epiphany that we must celebrate because Christ has become an incarnate member of our history. He wants to accompany every person, every family, every people. He wants to make the history of every Christian and every people a true salvation history.

Events of the Week

Therefore, sisters and brothers, when I speak to you about certain events, I am not discussing things that have nothing to do with the Church. My preaching must be framed by these realities.

For example, in our homily today, the feast of the baptism of Christ revealing himself as Savior, how can we ignore the fact that here in San Salvador this week people have been shaken by two contrasting articles in our newspapers? On the one hand, there was a rejection of the preaching and message of Father Robert Drinan, whom you heard here last week.[1] On the other hand, there was a presentation of the visit of the Human Rights Commission of the Organization of American States (OAS).[2]

I see a contrast between these two news items. The declarations of Father Robert Drinan leave many people scandalized and give others great hope, whereas the presence of the OAS is announced in ambivalent fashion: it awakens doubts and fears since it is made to appear that the commission is being manipulated. Father Drinan provokes scandal because he touches a sore spot. Moral theology speaks of three kinds of scandal. True scandal is that provoked by a sin or a fault; this is normal scandal, the real scandal that true evil produces in mature, sensible people. Another kind of scandal is the childish scandal produced in the faint-hearted, those who are scandalized by everything. A third type of scandal, that which is truly sinful, is the scandal of the Pharisees, the scandal of those who could not tolerate Christ. This is the scandal directed against people who try to point out injustices and disorders. You can draw your own conclusion about the type of scandal that is involved in the publication of these articles.

At the same time, people recognize the courage in the voice of priests who denounce things that the Church has continually denounced and who point out the real fears that exist in our people. For example, there are people who

---

1. In *La Prensa Gráfica* (January 13, 1978), two items were published under these titles: "Interior Ministry Rejects Accusation of Jesuit on Repression" and "Judgments of the Jesuit Drinan Considered Partial."

2. The Human Rights Commission of the Organization of American States (OAS), made up of Dr. Carlos A. Dunshee de Abranches, Dr. Fernando Volio, and Professor Tom J. Farer, visited El Salvador from January 11 to 18, 1978 to investigate the observance of human rights in the country.

should have presented themselves to the Human Rights Commission, but they did not have the courage to do so because they are afraid. What does that mean? It means that when Father Drinan speaks about the fear of the people and the *campesinos*, he is not lying. This is a reality that we see at this very moment. There are *campesinos* who ought to come forward but do not have the courage to do so.

Therefore I ask: How has this visit of the commission been presented? What reports have appeared in the newspapers portraying the victims of human rights violations? Who is reporting on other groups that have been assaulted? The reporting is biased. We could say that those who accused Father Drinan of speaking in a prejudiced way are doing the same thing with the OAS Commission: they are making it look partial. We hope that the human rights proponents in Latin America who are now present in El Salvador will speak with the same maturity and courage as Father Drinan did. We hope that they will rise above all intrigue and manipulation and know how to discover the truth by listening to those who should be heard.

They have asked for collaboration, and I want to tell you in the name of the Church that the voice of my office has always offered collaboration so that truth and justice are brought to light. Injustices have been denounced, and in light of these denunciations we ask the members of the OAS: Do you know how to respond to the question that arises from so many of our homes: Where are the disappeared? Just answering that would suffice. Just give this information to the many families who are suffering and do not know if their loved ones are alive or dead. Where are they? What is their situation?

This is the incarnation of Christ in our history and among our people. That is why it is painful, sisters and brothers, to present our poor country in this light, but when a picture comes out bad, the blame is not in the photography; it is in the object being portrayed.

We have also been saddened this week by the assassination of the journalist Doctor Pedro Joaquín Chamorro, and we join with the people of Nicaragua in lamenting his death. During our weekly interview on Wednesday we expressed our solidarity in suffering with the victim and his family and with the truth that he proclaimed. We also expressed our repudiation of every type of criminal activity.

Many letters from Amnesty International have arrived at our office inquiring about the situation of many prisoners, but I was especially moved by the questions concerning the case of the young woman Lil Milagro Ramírez. We also received letters from the families of Victor Manuel Rivas and Julio Antonio Ayala. The sentiments of these letters fill me with great emotion: "For us the voice of the Church is the voice of justice, the voice of those of us who are not heard." Thank you for understanding this, sisters and brothers, for the Church does not want to be anything else. Rather than a voice lost amid the tumult of distortion, confusion, and manipulation of the news, the Church wants to be the voice of those who have no voice.

Life of the Church

Moving on, sisters and brothers, in the name of Christ who desires "that all may be one" (John 17:21), I announce with joy the week of prayer for Christian unity. Protestants and Catholics have together prepared a program that appears in *Orientación* and will be read here in a short time. We will celebrate the traditional week of prayer from January 18 to 25. I make an appeal to all you Catholics and also to you, dear Protestant sisters and brothers. I know that you listen to me, and I'm so grateful when you tell me that you listen with great devotion—thank you! If we truly love Christ and the Gospel, then, I invite you to pray devoutly that this scandal of division among Christians be eliminated from the world. This division among Christians prevents Christ from being known, whereas unity among Christians would give great credibility to Christ's Church. Let us not be a hindrance, dear Protestants and Catholics. Let us unite in one faith as Christ desired: one single flock beneath the divine staff of the one Pastor (John 10:16).

I have not had the opportunity to thank and congratulate all those who made possible the World Day of Peace. The event left behind very profound and noble echoes, and these alone bespeak gratitude and recognition. But recalling these unforgettable celebrations, I do want to remind you to read and reflect on the New Year pastoral message that some of us bishops have published.[3] Also, the members of the National Commission for Peace and Justice have published their commentary on Pope Paul VI's message: "Yes to Peace! No to Violence!."

I have not had the opportunity, sisters and brothers, to read you a telegram message that arrived recently from the archbishop of Tegucigalpa, whom we were hoping to have here. We invited him, but he wrote, "I am sad that I cannot accept your kind invitation, but I wish you much success during this seminar on peace." As a sign of our fraternity, the priests from our seminary traveled to Tegucigalpa to participate in a course for seminary personnel. When they presented a birth-

---

3. Message signed by Archbishop Óscar A. Romero, Bishop Arturo Rivera Damas, and Bishop Marco René Revelo. See *Orientación* (January 8, 1978).

day cake to Archbishop Santos of Tegucigalpa, he told them, "Please take half the cake to the archbishop of San Salvador as a sign of unity." His words reflect what I said previously about the Lord of Esquipulas: the Church in Central America is united. It is politics that spoils this unity. Hopefully one day we will live out this faith that Christ proclaimed to us: ". . . that all may be one" (John 17:21).

The time has arrived for our schools to open their doors once again. I want to remind the Catholic schools that they should meditate profoundly on the recent document that was published by the Sacred Congregation for Catholic Education.[4] You know that the Church watches over the pastoral work of Catholic schools through a congregation, a body that might be compared to a government ministry. The pope exercises his teaching role through the Catholic schools. I would like to remind you of some phrases that appear in the document: the Catholic school is a means of serving the "Church's saving mission"; it is a means for "promoting the formation of the whole person, since the school is a center in which a specific concept of the world, of the human person, and of history is developed and conveyed."

"One must recognize that the work of a Catholic school is infinitely more complex and more difficult than ever before since this is a time when Christianity demands to be clothed in fresh garments, when all manner of changes have been introduced in the Church and in secular life, and particularly, when a pluralist mentality dominates and the Christian Gospel is increasingly pushed to the side lines." These words of the pope demand that Catholic schools put aside any tra-

---

4. Sacred Congregation for Catholic Education, "The Catholic School" (March 19, 1977). Full text published in *L'Osservatore Romano* (July 31, 1977). The quotations that follow are from this text.

ditions that separate them from the Church's teaching. They must not accommodate themselves so as to please certain sectors; rather, they must be messengers of the Church's truth for our changing times.

The true mission of the schools, says the document, is "to cooperate more closely with the apostolate of the bishops, both in the field of religious instruction and in the more general Christian education which they endeavor to promote by assisting people to a personal integration of culture and faith and of faith with living." This is the objective of a Catholic school. Let us avoid those shameful situations where students graduate from our schools having learned about the faith but then fail to translate this faith into action and so create unjust, sinful situations and other disorders of a corrupt society. If a Catholic school wants to be a missionary of the Church, it must remember that every mission must be connected to and in communion with the Church's teaching. That is why the document says that "the Catholic school receives from the bishops in some manner the "mandate" of an apostolic undertaking" and must be in communion with the hierarchy. It is impossible to conceive of a Catholic school that wishes to follow a line different from the Church's teaching. Let us keep this in mind so that we know whether to consider a school as truly Catholic or not.

Finally, sisters and brothers, I want to speak with delight about the exuberant religious life in our own Church. During these days we have established the Bethlehemite Sisters in a mission in El Paraíso and the Sisters of the Assumption in Chalatenango, where they will attend to Potonico. Very soon the Guadalupana Sisters will go to Arcatao. A course of adaptation is being prepared to train people for this new mission that the Church is entrusting to the sisters. We also had the pleasure of greeting several superiors general who visited El Salvador during these days: the superior general of the Dominican Sisters of the Annunciation who work in Santa Tecla, Suchitoto, and Quezaltepeque; the superior general of the Oblates of the Sacred Heart who work in the Colegio Sagrado Corazón, in Aguilares, in Lourdes, and in Dulce Nombre de María; and the superior general of the Oblates of Divine Love, who work in the Colegio La Sagrada Familia and the María Dimagio Catholic School and do pastoral ministry in Citalá.

As you can see, sisters and brothers, the Gospel message is becoming incarnate in so many ways that we rejoice to think of how truly alive our Church is, prolonging the mystery of Christ in El Salvador. Preaching this homily, therefore, is very easy. Today's readings present us with three priceless thoughts that we should absorb so that as Christians we will come to a greater understanding of the mystery of Christ as we move through this liturgical year. The first thought is that God wants to save everyone. The second is what Saint Paul writes in his letter: God wants to save us by forming a people on this earth. And the third thought is that God saves people by taking away the sins of the world. The Gospel presents Christ being baptized and presented as the "Lamb of God who takes away the sins of the world."

God Wants to Save Everyone

Our first thought is based on the words of the prophet Isaiah, who speaks in very poetic passages about the Servant of Yahweh. Who is this Servant of God? This remains a mystery: it might be some mysterious person, or it could refer to the people of Israel, but in any case it is a prophecy that points to Jesus Christ, the true Servant of God. This Servant of God is given a mission: to bring together the scant forces of the people who now live scattered in exile. God tells him, "Is it a small task for you to be my servant, to reestablish the tribes of Jacob, and restore the remnant of Israel? I will make you a light to the nations so you can bring my deliverance to the far ends of the earth" (Isa 49:6).

How this fills us with joy, sisters and brothers! Living here in El Salvador in 1978, we are confronted by this universal vision of God in Christ. "I make you the salvation of all the ends of the earth." Here on this feast of the Lord of Esquipulas, the crucified Christ is present in Central America and in our diocese. He is the Servant of God, the Christ who we believe has gathered us together in this Mass. He is present in all the communities that gather to meditate on these words. As the Council tells us, Christ becomes present in the words of the priest who preaches, in the mystery celebrated on the altar, in the Communion we receive, in the sacraments that purify us (*Sacrosanctum Concilium* 7). Christ is the Servant of God saving all the ends of the earth.

We ought to be filled with enthusiasm to know that no one, not one of us, is excluded from salvation. God calls everyone, and therefore the Church cries out for justice and rejects the scandal of the Pharisees; she repudiates violence, lies, crimes, and persecution. But she never cries out for vengeance; she always speaks with love and calls sinners to repentance, for God desires to save them. God invites those who have killed and slandered and persecuted to return to him. They are the prodigal sons whom the father is waiting to save (Luke 15:20).

I am very happy, sisters and brothers, that my enemies listen to me. You who are faithful and listen to me with love and devotion, please pardon me for saying this, but my enemies are listening to me because I speak to them words of love. I do not hate them, nor do I seek revenge. I wish them no harm. I ask them to be converted and to be blessed with the blessedness you have, for you possess the joy of your faith, like the son in the parable who was always with his father (Luke 15:31). Yesterday a friend of mine affectionately told me, "I hope you know that all the good folks are with you." My sisters and brothers, I don't know how to distinguish between good and bad people. You are all children of God, and the Lord loves you all. Today's readings present us with a universal call to salvation.

God Wants to Save Us by Forming a People on This Earth

My second thought is that God wants to save us as a people. He does not want to save each of us in isolation. That is why the Church today more than ever before emphasizes what it means to be a "people." And that is why the Church experiences conflicts: the Church does not want just crowds; she wants a people. A crowd is a bunch of individuals, and the more lethargic they are, the better; the more conformist they are, the better. The Church rejects the communist propaganda that religion is the opium of the people. She has no intention of being the opium of the people. It is others who drug the people and put them to sleep, and they are happy to keep them that way.

The Church wants to rouse men and women to the true meaning of being a people. What does it mean to be a people? A people is a community of persons in which everyone works together for the common good. And what is the common good? The Council states, "The common good is the sum of those conditions of social life which allow social groups and their individual members relatively thorough and ready access to their own development" (*Gaudium et Spes 26*).

A society's or a political community's reason for existence is the human person, not the security of the state. When Christ said, "The Sabbath was made for man, not man for the Sabbath" (Mark 2:27), he was stating the principle that all laws and all institutions exist for the sake of human beings. The human person is not for the state; rather, the state is for the human person. The development of humanity depends upon our concept of the human person.

I want to read you this incomparable passage from Pope Paul VI's encyclical, *Populorum Progressio*. In his recent discourse to our ambassador, the pope applied to Salvadorans these words that you can read in *Populorum Progressio*, number 20: "This is what will guarantee man's authentic development: his transition from less human conditions to truly human ones." Do you see? It is not some mass of people; it is the transition of each and every person to more human conditions.

The pope describes these conditions in his encyclical, and we should keep them in mind because they define what it means to be a people. When they are not realized for every Salvadoran, then the people suffer "less human conditions, such as the lack of material goods that are necessary for at least a minimum standard of living." Less human conditions also exist when people "experience a moral poverty that results from selfishness, and even less human are those oppressive structures that arise from the abuse of wealth or the abuse of power, from the exploitation of workers and the injustice of transactions" (*Populorum Progressio* 21). These are all less human conditions. Don't you think that they refer to certain realities here in El Salvador?

The passage to more human conditions is also described by the pope: "The rise from poverty to the acquisition of life's necessities; the elimination of social ills; broadening the horizons of knowledge; acquiring refinement and culture. From there one can go on to acquire a growing awareness of other people's dignity, a taste for the spirit of poverty" (*Populorum Progressio* 21). It is admirable that the Church places this spirit of poverty here among the more human conditions. Being poor and having a spirit of poverty is not underdevelopment; it is human development. The more people live this spirit of poverty, the more human they become. The more they are victims of avarice, the less morally developed they are.

The pope continues, "More human conditions include an active interest in the common good and a desire for peace." And still more human are those "persons who can acknowledge the highest values and God himself, their author and end. Finally and above all, there is faith—God's gift to people of good will—and our growing unity in Christ, who calls God the Father of all people" (*Populorum Progressio* 21). What a beautiful description of what it means to be a people! The day that we Salvadorans escape from this accumulation of less human conditions and move toward personal and national conditions that are more human—by which we mean not only economic development but the spirit of faith and adoration of the one and only God—then that will be the true development of our people.

The reading from Saint Paul speaks to us about the "Church of God in Corinth" (1 Cor 1:2). We can speak instead about the Church of God in El Salvador or the Church of God in each nation where priests and bishops work together for human development. This is not subversion or communism or a desire to gain power. We respect temporal power, but we want to create in people's consciousness a feeling of being a people, not just a crowd. We seek the development of individuals and a type of well-being that violates no one's rights but cultivates love and faith among all who are children of the Father of all.

Because the Church preaches this development of the human person, she has been maligned. Where the Church refrains from this kind of preaching, she has no problems. That is why I say to all of you who are pastoral ministers—priests, religious, Catholic schools, pastoral movements: we have to follow the line that Saint Paul sets down for us. We have to form the Church of God as the community Christ wants: a community inspired by his love to become the ferment of a pluralist society. The Church does not want everyone to become Catholic, but she wants Catholics to be true missionaries of this message of development and to promote unity, development, light, and also criticism. The Church wants people to have a critical consciousness and to be aware of the different ways of thinking in a pluralist society for this is the diversity that God desires. We should not judge everyone with the same criteria; rather, the beauty of pluralism in our own Salvadoran reality should enhance us as humans and strengthen the unity of our nation.

God Saves People by Taking Away the Sins of the World

Finally, sisters and brothers, my third thought: Jesus is presented in the River Jordan as the Lamb of God who takes away the sins of the world. "He existed before I did," says John the Baptist. "I am announcing him because the salvation of humankind consists in receiving the baptism of the Spirit that he brings" (John 1:30, 33). Jesus wants to instill the life of God into people's hearts so that they will be renewed interiorly, and in this way he takes away the sins of people, of families, of society. This is the mission entrusted to the Church, a difficult mission: to uproot sins from history, to uproot sins from politics, to uproot sins from the economy, to uproot sins from wherever they are. What a difficult task!

The Church has to confront conflicts caused by great self-ishness, great pride, and great vanity because so many people have enthroned the kingdom of sin among us. The Church must suffer for speaking the truth, for denouncing sin, and for uprooting sin. No one wants to have a sore spot touched, and therefore a society with so many sores reacts strongly when someone has the courage to touch the sore and say, "You have to treat that. You have to eliminate that. Believe in Christ and be converted!" Christ alone can take away the sins of our Salvadoran society and create a genuine community of people, and of such a community God will be truly proud because God has created the diverse peoples as one family.

How wonderful it is to think of God as the Father of all peoples who live according to God's ways and who love one another in this pluralism of nations! What a great diversity of characteristics! Just think of the countries of Central America as five children of God, each one with its own distinctiveness. How marvelous it would be if these five nations, freed from the sins of their history, their politics, and their conflicts, were to present themselves on this feast of the Lord of Esquipulas as brothers and sisters of Christ. As peoples devoted to God, they would move from inhuman conditions to conditions worthy of God's children and would become images of his presence in this small territory known as Central America!

Dear sisters and brothers, do you see now how the incarnation of Christ, born in Bethlehem and revealed in the Epiphany, has to be the bright light that illuminates our reality in El Salvador? As Salvadorans and as Church, we are going to hope for these things as we say our Creed.

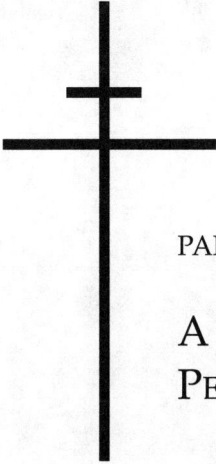

PART IV

A Prophetic and Persecuted People

The Mission of the Prophets

(August 14, 1977)

It is impossible to distill Romero's preaching to one theme or one idea. However, perhaps the closest would be his goal of articulating what it means to be the true Church of Jesus Christ. But "articulate" is too weak here. Romero's goal wasn't simply to provide a good, clear theology of the Church. He wanted his people to grow ever more fully into *being* the Church, into living out their identity as the people of God in El Salvador. In the midst of confusions, competing ideologies, and violence, he urged all—including himself—to put the Gospel at the center of their lives and feel the responsibility for living it out. Romero never wanted a passive people who simply entrusted the mission of the Church to him and the clergy. Among his people, he saw thousands of ordinary laypersons already taking up their call to build up God's kingdom; Romero urged everyone to do the same.

In an early homily from Holy Thursday, 1977, Romero sets the theological foundations for this call. Here he takes up a central teaching of Vatican II: that every Christian, whatever their state of life, is called to the fullness of Christian love and to a full participation in the mission of the Church. The clergy and religious do not represent a higher or holier path. Instead, at baptism, every Christian receives the foundational call to partake in Christ's priestly, prophetic, and kingly work. Romero wanted his people to respond to this call. A passage from this early homily is worth quoting at length:

> Today's Mass began with that hymn from the Book of Revelation placed on the lips of all of us: "You made us a priestly people, a royal people, and a prophetic people because the anointing of the Spirit who anointed Christ is also ours" (Rev 1:6b). On the day of our baptism, dear sisters and brothers, when the water and the Spirit cleansed us from original sin, the priest showed the greatness of this moment by anointing our heads with the sacred chrism that we are going to consecrate here [during this Chrism Mass]. Through this anointing we show that baptism incorporates the child of the flesh into the Church, which is the people of God, a priestly people, a people of prophets and kings. This is a blessed time to remember our own baptism. This is the time for the priests and for all of us to renew the commitments which flow from our anointing. I would like to invite you, dear sisters and brothers, to call to mind the chrism that each of you received at the baptismal font of your town or village. There we were born; there the priest came with both the waters of baptism and with the holy chrism brought from the cathedral and consecrated that year to anoint the members of this priestly, royal, prophetic people
>
> As the people of God, therefore, we have this threefold responsibility and this threefold honor which, thanks be to God, lay people are coming to

understand more and more. You are neither religious nor priests of the altar, but you are priests in the world, you are prophets in the world, and you are kings and queens who must work so that the kingdom of Christ reigns in society and in the structures of the world. Like the prophets, you, as a prophetic people anointed by the Spirit who anointed Christ, have to announce the marvelous deeds of God in the world. You have to encourage the good that is done in the world and emphatically denounce the evil that is done in the world. That is what prophets are for: to announce and encourage goodness and to denounce and condemn evil. You, as a people blessed with the powerful anointing of the Spirit, are understanding this more and more so that you should not look only to the bishop or the priests to see what they are doing, but rather you yourselves should feel responsible for this priestly, royal, and prophetic Church.

I am very happy, sisters and brothers, to share these reflections with you and to remember our common baptism. There are already many communities in our diocese that are becoming more aware of this meaning of baptism. There are many communities where people are living out this responsibility to be members of the Church, members of the people of God anointed with the paschal power of our Lord Jesus Christ. Let us keep working and becoming more aware that we are not simply spectators of the Church's activity. Let us feel that we are Church, because indeed we are Church, because the Spirit of God has anointed us and enabled us to carry out, like Christ, a priestly mission that consecrates the world to God, a prophetic mission that announces God to the world, and a royal mission that makes Christ reign over all that exists on earth. (April 7, 1977)

Seen from a certain perspective, Romero's preaching over the next three years was no more than a weekly remembrance of this idea: "let us feel that we are Church"; let us live out the priestly, prophetic, and royal calling entrusted to each person. What a beautiful message. Certainly, this was felt as a message of welcome and inclusion—each one of you represents the Church. But even more it was a call to responsibility and mission: go forth, *be* the Church, consecrate every inch of the world to God, announcing God's truth and denouncing sins, building God's kingdom in every time and place.

Romero preached many times on each dimension of this calling. We already saw a glimpse of his vision of the priestly calling of every Christian in his funeral homily for Rutilio Grande, Manuel Solórzano, and Nelson Lemus. In that moment, he lifted them up as examples of true Christian liberators, as Christians, we could say, whose work sanctifies the world. He pointed to three dimensions of such a life: grounded in faith, guided by social teaching, and oriented by love. These martyrs demonstrated true holiness, the true priestly calling of all. We've also seen aspects of Romero's theology of the kingdom of God, particularly in his continual insistence that we avoid the two extremes of spiritualistic escape and materialistic reduction. We'll continue to see him develop this vision in the homilies to come.

The next three homilies, however, focus on Romero's insistence on the prophetic calling of the Christian community. This theme runs deep in his homiletic corpus. As you will see, the ultimate aim of the prophet is *conversion*, a turning away from sin and a turning toward God. It would be hard to overemphasize the importance of this movement for Romero. As he once said, "I will never grow weary of shouting this word 'conversion'" (August 21, 1977)! This call, as Romero further explains, is nothing other than the invitation to each of us—including to Romero himself—to continually turn more fully toward God. Encouraging and demanding such movement is the work of the prophet.

Looking deeper, one finds repeated in Romero's preaching that this prophetic work has a two-sided quality: to *announce* the Gospel and to *denounce* sin. The former, of course, is primary. To go forth and announce the good news, to point to how God is working here and now, and to encourage everyone to do what it is good is at the heart of the Christian life. But look around: not all is good. And the path forward must be an honest recognition of that fact. A cheerful ignorance of sin will not do. Thus, to truly proclaim the Good News to the world, the prophet must also denounce sin, denounce all the ways in which the world does not yet conform to God's plan.

Romero's homily of August 14, 1977 represents a sort of initial "theology of the prophet." Here you will see his strong insistence on the dual work of annunciation and denunciation. Many other moments in the homily may strike you, but I will highlight two that stand out for me. First, Romero offers a wonderful explanation of the concept of "peace" as it is understood within Catholic social teaching. This moment is also typical of Romero's preaching. As he already insisted in the first homily included in this book, Romero saw in Catholic social teaching a clear guide to announcing the fullness of the Gospel and to denouncing sin.

Here he focuses on a true vision of peace grounded in justice. But he might just as well have explored—as he does elsewhere—our shared human dignity, the common good, true solidarity, or the meaning of created goods.

Second, Romero points in the homily toward a fuller account of sin than many Christians are used to. Sin is certainly a reality within the individual person, and thus Romero notes how each one of us is called to continual conversion. However, sin is also a social reality. Romero saw this all around him: political structures that violated basic human rights, economic structures marginalizing and oppressing the poor, and a culture of greed that closed off the hearts of the rich to the suffering of their brothers and sisters.

In this homily, Romero connects the work of prophetic denunciation to the religious language of "idolatry." An idol is anything we make our ultimate love and hope in place of God. The prophet must denounce such idolatry *and* reveal how it is never just a personal affair. As he will speak of the idol of money two months later, "The people are adoring it and prostrating themselves before it and offering sacrifices to it. What incredible sacrifices are made to this idol of money, and not only sacrifices but even iniquities. People are paid to kill; sin is bought and sold; everything is commercialized; with money everything is licit" (September 11, 1977). When society is in such a place, the prophet must denounce the idol and announce the Gospel. That's exactly what Romero does in this homily.

Suggestions for Further Reading

The next two homilies in this book will further explore Romero's vision of the prophetic work of the Church and of every Christian. As already noted, a key foundation of this work for Romero is Catholic social teaching. His homilies focused on particular aspects of Catholic social teaching thus provide crucial examples of his own taking up of the prophetic work of the preacher.

- "The Proper Use of the Goods that God has Created" (September 25, 1977) in *A Prophetic Bishop Speaks to His People: The Complete Homilies of Archbishop Óscar Arnulfo Romero*, 6 vols., trans. Joseph Owens, SJ (Convivium Press, 2015–2016), 1.321–332.

- "No to Violence! Yes to Peace!" (January 6, 1978) in *A Prophetic Bishop Speaks*, 2.178–184.

Sunday, August 14, 1977
Mass Readings
Jeremiah 38:4–6, 8–10; Hebrews 12:1–4
Luke 12:49–53

. . . [we] share with you the concerns, joys, and hopes of the diocese, just as we also share in the problems of all of you.[1] May the word of God, the true path we must follow, shed light on this reality of our history.

Life of the Church

Tomorrow is the great day of Mary's assumption in body and soul into heaven. This triumphal ascent of Mary after a life of commitment to God is in itself a message. Let us try to go to Holy Mass if we have time or at least spend some time in our homes reflecting on this our Mother. Even though being assumed into heaven and constituted Queen of the Universe, she still always has her eyes set on this earth. She is concerned about our life, and this should give us great reason for trust and hope, for Mary is crowned in heaven as a reward for her virtues.

At 11 o'clock in the morning we will have a Mass here during which Jorge Benavides, a young man who has completed his theological studies, will be ordained a deacon. On this occasion of the feast of the Assumption we want to

---

1. The greeting and opening words are not recorded on the tape of this homily.

congratulate the Catholics of the parish in Mejicanos where they celebrate the Virgin as their patroness. We also congratulate the Religious of the Assumption, who celebrate their principal feast on August 15.

I also want to communicate to you and ask you to pray for the priests and religious who are directly involved in the pastoral work in the villages. We are going to meet together on Tuesday, Wednesday, and Thursday to study a document written by Pope Paul VI that I would like everyone to become familiar with. Like other Church documents, this one receives its name from the first two words of the Latin version, since Latin is the official language of the Church. The pope writes these documents in Latin, and they are then translated into other languages, but they continue to be known by their first two Latin words. This document is called *Evangelii Nuntiandi* and deals with evangelization in today's world.[2] It brings together the results of a grand consultation that the pope made in 1974 with all the bishops of the world. The Church is concerned with bringing her eternal message to the modern-day world which can seem so complicated and difficult. We will examine these very wise guidelines set down by the world's bishops and the pope as supreme teacher in the Church, and we will deepen our knowledge of them so that our evangelization in the archdiocese corresponds to a whole series of wonderful initiatives. We hope, therefore, that all the priests and women religious doing direct pastoral work will unify their criteria and make known their difficulties so that no one feels that there are two Churches here in the diocese. The impression is sometimes given that certain people criticize the attitudes

---

2. Recall that this is the same text that Romero references in the two homilies at the beginning of this book.

and the criteria of the archbishop and the priests who are with him, as if they were part of some other Church and were able to criticize the hierarchical Church. This is not the time for such disunity. This is a time for dialogue, and now we have these three days to dialogue in depth. In those matters where we disagree, let us see if we are mistaken. It is not a matter of imposing anything capriciously but of carrying out our great evangelizing task with criteria which, even if not pleasing to the world, are pleasing to God and to the souls who want to be faithful to the plan of God.

I also announce to you joyfully that next week, God willing, I will have ready the pastoral letter that I announced to you on August 6. This letter deals with the Church as the Body of Christ in history; that is, it explains how the Church in every age simply does what Jesus himself would do at that time. If Jesus were a Salvadoran in 1977, what would he do? That is what the Church asks, and that is what the Church does.

I also want to share with you a concern of several Christian communities who are protesting what happened to the catechist Filomena Portillo Puerta, a young woman of twenty-one years who was captured on July 30 in Ciudad Delgado and found dead in Tejulta, Chalatenango. What is happening here? Are things getting better, or do they remain the same? Also, a catechist of Father Salvador Colorado in Ciudad Delgado was captured, tortured, and threatened with death along with Father Colorado. As a result, Father Colorado has suffered an emotional crisis and is being treated. This also is persecution.

We ask for any news about those who have been imprisoned and disappeared. The Church cannot refrain from expressing her solidarity with human rights and with the suffering of families who see their loved ones disappear. The

Church cannot have confidence as long as there is no discussion of these deeds and no environment of greater trust.

I also want to announce to you that the documents of Medellín are now available. This effort of the Universidad José Simeón Cañas places the documents within reach of our people so that no Catholic today should be ignorant of them. Unfortunately, many people are learning about these documents through false lenses; they are distorted by biased publications which want the world to believe that the Church is Marxist. Many people have knowledge of the Medellín documents only through these poisonous columns. I believe that we can count on mature Catholics to have their own criteria and not believe things to be dogmas of faith just because they are printed in the newspapers or heard on television or radio. Go to the sources. Use your critical sense of things. When you read a newspaper, including the editorial pages, you have to use your judgment to say, "this is a lie" or "this seems to be biased." This is how you reveal the maturity of your judgment when you read or go to the movies. No film is bad if you have your own criteria and know how to condemn immorality and everything objectionable. There is no need for someone to tell you, "this is permitted for such and such an age." Your own criteria tell you this. Therefore, when dealing with the Medellín documents, it is necessary to know them in their sources, and these sources are now available to you. I asked them to bring copies to the cathedral today, and I suppose they will be available at the end of Mass. If not, look for them in Catholic bookstores or in the chancery offices.

There are more acts of violence, sisters and brothers, that have occurred during these days. The Church cannot accept violence in any form. These crimes and these captures and these tortures are acts of violence, just like the bomb that exploded in San Salvador and the kidnapping of Dr. Carlos Emilio Alvarez.[3] The Church cannot approve of any of these actions. Violence is inhuman. It does not build but destroys. It destroys above all our hopes for improvement. I beg you, then, with all the authority that the Church gives me before my beloved people: let us think with God, the God of peace, the God who loves us, the God who forgives all sinners if they repent.

One of the most beautiful letters that arrived this week reads thus: "What most amazes me about the Church during these days is that, despite all the attacks and even assassinations she has suffered, no words of hatred or vengeance have been heard from her, but always words of love and conversion." How well these humble souls grasp the Church's intentions! I am happy that people feel this way, even while others persist in calling the Church violent and saying she is the source of the wrongs being committed. Those who listen without prejudice and without selfish interests hear the Church's true language: we say "no" to violence, and we call sinners to be converted. I repeat what I said here on the day of Father Grande's funeral: "Who knows if the assassins of this victim are listening to me on the radio? Know that we do not hate you and that we pray to God that you repent and join us one day to receive the bread that God gives with a kiss of love even to sinners, even to murderers." What joy the Church would feel on the day when they are all converted: those who have written or paid others to write against the Church, those who have used arms to humiliate villages,

---

3. The Armed Forces of National Resistance (FARN) kidnapped Carlos Emilio Álvarez Geoffroy on August 11, 1977 and freed him eight days later, after their demands had been met. See *La Prensa Gráfica* (August 13 and 20, 1977).

those who have tortured people in brutal ways. Would that they see how wrong their actions are and repent and ask pardon of God who still awaits them. God certainly gives life to sinners, and he does so because he is waiting for them. I hope, dear friends, that you are listening to me, perhaps feeling humiliated because of what you have done, because violence is never something to be proud of. Those who beat others always feel ashamed; they are more humiliated than those they have beaten. Realize that this is truly shameful, above all in a country that calls itself civilized. If we truly want to beautify the face of our country, then let us wash our inner conscience, especially you who are culpable, you who are sponsors, you who tolerate and enable this situation that cannot continue.

In What Does Peace Consist?

And here we are now with the word of God, brothers and sisters. What I find in the message of the prophet Jeremiah and the letter to the Hebrews and above all in the divine words of Christ in his Gospel, is the secret of happiness. Perhaps some of you are surprised by how Christ presents himself today, saying, "Do you think that I have come to bring peace to the earth? No, but rather division" (Luke 12:51). Now don't go saying that Christ is preaching physical violence. He is indeed preaching violence, but it is the true violence that is needed for true peace. He tells people, "Don't think that I have come to bring a superficial peace."

This is the first point of today's message. In what does peace consist? Peace consists in being in harmony with the plan of God. When a life, a family, or a people is in harmony with the will of God, then there is true peace. In my pastoral letter I stress this concept. True peace occurs when the history of humankind faithfully reflects salvation history. There are not two histories. The history of human beings—of each person and of all those who form part of a nation—is not distinct from the history of salvation or the plan of God. That project that God proposes is similar to the plan that an architect presents for the construction of a building. As long as the contractor follows the architectural plans, the building will be solidly constructed. But if a foreman or some workers should happen to lay the foundation incorrectly or nail beams where they don't belong, then the plan of the architect is useless. The same can be said of God's plan for humankind and his history of salvation: if people decide to construct the world according to their selfish caprices and not according to the plan of God, then that plan is frustrated.

Peace, then, consists of knowing what God wants of this society, what God wants of my life, what God wants of the republic. And that should be the vision of government officials and all those who build up our society. The people who can change the destiny of the country with their money, their technology, and their political ability should follow God's plan and not just trust in their own impulses. As good builders they should be continually extending God's architectural plan for this nation and should build accordingly. Then there will be peace. As for the rest, it is as the Council says, "Peace is not merely the absence of war. Nor can it be reduced solely to the maintenance of a balance of power between enemies" (*Gaudium et Spes* 78). Above all, peace is not the sign of death in a repressive atmosphere where no one can speak; it is not the peace of cemeteries. True peace is based on justice, on equality, on the plan of God who has created us in his image and likeness and has given us all the ability to contribute to the common good of the republic. This ability is given not to some small group that God has chosen, but to all Salvadorans. We all have the right to participate in forging our own destiny and our own common good. This is our right as humans, and no one should be excluded.

When history is developed in this way, it is magnificent. When it coincides with the history of salvation, then there is peace. This is a very profound reality and not everyone understands it. That is why Christ says division will arise as a result of this doctrine. "A household of five will be divided, three against two and two against three," says Christ. Even among family members, a daughter and a mother will be in disagreement because one understands true peace and the other wants a false peace (Luke 12:52–53). One person understands the meaning of true peace and another wants a superficial peace. In any society there will be division as long as certain people, stubbornly determined to have their own way, seek to establish peace on the basis of injustices, self-interests, repression, and violation of rights. Peace is not built that way. There will be a false peace, not the peace that Christ gives us. "My peace I give you", says the risen Christ, "but not as the world gives it" (John 14:27). The world is falsely irenic when there is the mere appearance of peace: we shake hands, but we know that we have very different ideas. In former times there were greater social sanctions so that people behaved differently. They had such a sense of their nobility that if a murderer or a thief arrived, even if he were a great lord, they would not shake his hand because to shake hands meant that one was in full accord with the other. Would that this noble sense of social sanction were restored in our society so that we could make claims against those who are not in agreement with the plan of God. Yes, we must respect their way of thinking, but we must also understand that they are not establishing true peace, and this is where conflicts arise.

The Prophets Announce God's Plan

The role of the prophets is the second consideration of this homily, and we can understand the prophet's role by looking at the central figure of the first reading, Jeremiah, and the central figure of the second reading, Jesus Christ. Jeremiah was one of the finest figures foreshadowing the mission of Christ. Just as Christ, for preaching true peace that went against the selfish caprices of the powerful, died crucified on a cross, so Jeremiah was also a man of sorrows. For about fifty years his prophetic mission was nothing but pain and tribulation, and it reached its peak in the reading we heard today. His enemies obtained authorization from the king to throw Jeremiah into a cistern, a deep well. Another man, however, had influence with the weak king, Zedekiah, and he got a countervailing order to remove the prophet from the well. Jeremiah trusted in God, and God saved his life (Jer 38:10). Those of you who like to read the Bible, I recommend that you read the book of Jeremiah this week. A very interesting book! But read it above all in its historical context. For a while, during the reign of Josiah, Jeremiah was happy because the king and the prophet worked together, trying to restore the true image of God among the people of God. This was the king's duty. When the prophet saw the king's good will and his positive attitudes in defending the rights of God, he gave his approval to the king and supported him.

The Church is not fighting with the government. She is only saying that, like King Josiah, the government should look to God and do what God wants. This is the role of the prophets in the Old and the New Testaments: to announce the plan of God. When people accept this plan, there are no conflicts; there is rather joy. The prophet Jeremiah hoped that it would be that way always, but when King Josiah died, Jehoiakim became king and then Zedekiah, who appears in today's reading. That was when the conflicts began, because the kings allowed the people to prostitute themselves with their idolatry. They drew away from God and worshiped false gods. Even the temple priests were condemned. At that time the prophets were distinct from the priestly class and could therefore criticize the priests for being servants of the powerful and too secure in their religion. They told the priests, "Don't rely on having the temple of God. If you do not conduct yourselves according to the will of God, you are offending your Lord, and this temple will be destroyed, and the armies of Babylon will come and destroy Jerusalem, and the leaders of the people will be led into exile for a second time" (Jer 7:1–15). These words disturbed the idolaters because here was a man who wanted to purify the history of God in the people. A prophet is bound to disturb a society when the society is not in accord with God and the prophet calls it to account. That is what happened with Jeremiah: he became estranged from the people. They did not like him, as you heard in today's first reading: "This Jeremiah should die! He is demoralizing the soldiers and all the people with his discourses. He is not interested in the welfare of the people, but in their ruin" (Jer 38:4). See how the accusations against the prophets of every age are the same. When the prophet disturbs the selfish consciences of those who are not building according to God's plans, then he is a nuisance and must be eliminated, murdered, thrown into a pit. He must be persecuted and not allowed to speak his bothersome words. But the prophet could not speak otherwise. Read in the Bible, and you will see how often Jeremiah prayed to God, "Lord, take this cross from me. I do not want to be a prophet. I feel my insides burning because I have to say things even I don't like to say" (Jer 20:9).

The Prophets Call People to Conversion

It's always the same, sisters and brothers: the prophet has to denounce society's sin and call people to conversion, just as the Church is doing today in San Salvador. She denounces everything that would enthrone sin in El Salvador's history, and she calls sinners to be converted, just as Jeremiah did: "Reform your ways and your deeds! If you do not, this temple in which you trust will be destroyed. Reform your ways and your deeds! The armies from the north are coming and will carry us off into exile" (Jer 26:1–13). This was the political situation. Palestine wanted to seek support from Egypt, but God had another plan. How terrible are God's plans when people do not want to obey God of their own accord! There are men in world history who are sadly famous because they were chosen by God to be the scourges of sinful society. Could this not be our own situation? Are our overseers the scourges of our society? God needs such people, unfortunately, because people do not want to be converted of their own accord. But God hopes, as does the prophet, that with the people's conversion happiness will once again arrive. God hopes even when he knows that misfortune will come, and come it did. They destroyed the temple, and its walls are still there as testimony.

Now that the Israelis are in possession of Jerusalem, Jewish people from all over the world return to weep at those walls of Jerusalem for they recall this passage from Jeremiah. The people did not want to obey. As a result they had to perish and go into exile in Babylon. They lived humiliated under foreign rule through their own fault, because of their social sin and their idolatry. They suffered because of the failure of their authorities to call the people to order and because of the sins of injustice that Jeremiah denounced. The people felt secure in their old religious traditions and did not renew them. They did not pay heed to the will of God until their priests were deported, and the priests themselves were servile and flattering toward the king, the army, and the people who wanted to continue their idolatry.

God also punishes priests when they do not fulfill their obligations. We have said before that this denunciation of sin also includes us priests. We also are sinners, and we ask God's forgiveness. In my pastoral letter I say that the Church has come to a better understanding of the world in order to question the world about its sins, but at the same time the Church must question herself about her own ecclesiastical sins. We are human and capable of sin, and we have need of conversion. We call the people to turn not toward us but toward God, for we must all be converted toward God. God's plan can also be disrupted by us, the bishops and priests. What the kingdom of God demands of the Church and the world is universal transformation.

The Prophets also Announce Hope

But there is always hope—and here I end my humble commentary on today's word. The prophets announced disasters, and the disasters came, but the prophets also proclaimed a time of hope. In the midst of his lamentations, Jeremiah announces that this people, once reformed, will return to their land. In fact, he says something very beautiful about those being persecuted. Jeremiah places his hope especially in those who are exiled; he says this remnant of Israel will set an example in Palestine because they were faithful to God's word (Jer 31:1–7). They offer hope that this message will not fall on deaf ears.

I have great hope, my sisters and brothers, because I know that the words of these Sunday homilies touch many hearts. I hope that people understand the intention of my words: they are a denunciation of sin that the Church can never tolerate, not even in her members, and they are a call to conversion from sin. We all have to examine our lives in depth—priests, religious, Catholic schools, Church institutions, pious associations—all of us, beginning with the archbishop, have to examine our lives to see we if we are living in accord with God's will. We must then confront the world with a witness of holiness, as did Jeremiah who backed up his witness with his life. That is how we must live even when living this way brings outrages upon us.

I congratulate all those catechists and preachers of the word of God who despite the persecution remain faithful like Jeremiah. There is hope, and Jeremiah revealed this hope with a dramatic gesture, for like all the prophets he spoke not only with words but also with gestures. . . .[4]

---

4. The final words are not recorded on the tape of this homily.

The Church: A Prophetic, Sacramental, Community of Love

(September 10, 1978)

The prophetic call of the Church means that the Christian community cannot remain indifferent to the world around it. As a famous line from Vatican II proclaims, the Church in every age must take up the task of "scrutinizing the signs of the times and of interpreting them in the light of the Gospel" (*Gaudium et Spes* 4). The Church must ever discern the ways in which God is moving in the world, but a world in which sin remains stubbornly present. By the fall of 1978 in El Salvador, the prophetic task of announcing the Good News, calling for true peace, and denouncing sin had become more difficult and more dangerous. The violence and polarization seemed to increase every day.

By summer of 1978, the divisions within society at large were also open and evident within the Church. The oligarchical elite, who had come to expect a relationship of mutual support with the bishops of the country, now felt rejected by the archbishop. Romero insisted he had rejected no one, but his words fell on deaf ears.

Romero continued his refusal to attend public government events, as announced in the wake of the murder of Rutilio Grande (and the ongoing lack of any real investigation). Although he kept the lines of communication open as a way of seeking peace, he withdrew the traditional support for the government that bishops had often given. He insisted again and again that he was not an opponent of the government; he was not a political partisan on the other side. He simply wasn't willing to stay silent in the face of the violation of human rights. Furthermore, it is worth noting that Romero's preaching bothered the revolutionary movements on the left as well. He was clearly sympathetic with their demand for social change. And he also clearly saw these movements as driven by the clear good of the people, in contrast to the forces of repressive violence seeking to defend an oppressive status quo. There was not a moral equivalence in his mind. Nevertheless, various revolutionary groups found Romero, particularly in his continual rejection of violence, to be too passive, too slow. In the face of all these groups and challenges, Romero insisted that the only "side" he would take was with the flourishing of the people and the building of true peace grounded in justice.

It is important to remember here that the vast majority of Salvadorans in Romero's time were baptized Catholics. Conflict in society often represented a conflict in the pews —and among those at the altar, as the six bishops of the country were deeply divided as well. At first, subtly and hidden from view, but, by the summer and fall of 1978, the divisions were scandalously out in the open. Put simply, four of Romero's fellow bishops opposed his vision for the Church. They did not publicly support the furthest extremes on the right—the pamphlet, for example, that declared, "Be a patriot, kill a priest"—but at times they came close, as when some of them publicly stated that martyred priests such as Rutilio Grande and Alfonso Navarro had been meddling in politics. Despite Romero's regular and vigorous rejections of violence, these bishops saw little difference between his prophetic stance on behalf of the poor and the Marxist revolutionaries seeking to violently overthrow the government. In short, they were sympathetic with the accusation that Romero and many of these priests had become Marxists. They disagreed with Romero's stance towards the government, the length and content of his homilies, and the general direction in which he was taking the archdiocese.

This opposition went so far that in the summer of 1978 they wrote to Rome to have Romero removed as archbishop. In response, Romero sent a dossier of documents to the Vatican and traveled in June to meet with Vatican officials and the pope. In some meetings, Romero was distressed by how strongly the narrative of his fellow bishops had taken hold; but in others, he was encouraged. And then he met with Pope Paul VI. In the pope he found someone who understood him and what he was doing in El Salvador; Paul VI told Romero to remain courageous, to go forward with encouragement, patience, strength, and hope. Romero came home to El Salvador invigorated in his ministry. He was still strongly committed to bringing unity within the Church and among the bishops. But he also understood that sometimes the prophet must also speak to the Church itself. The prophet's call to conversion is not only an outward call to society. It first goes forth to the Christian community itself.

The bishops were particularly divided by how to respond to the rise of the "popular organizations" which increasingly dominated Salvadoran society. These groups struggled for the future of the country. The "popular organizations" included a wide variety of movements and associations that were in some way involved in the social and political life of the country. Reform-minded groups of rural laborers—often originating out of parishes and other small Christian communities—organized for land reform and other social change. Labor unions of all sorts pushed for new laws. There were also more strident and active revolutionary movements. And responding to all of these were reactionary movements on the right. These groups had long policed the society to maintain the status quo. They maintained both a network of spies among the rural poor and active paramilitary groups that committed some of the most heinous acts of repression and violence.

Clear to everyone was the instability of the situation. The challenge was how to respond. Was the way forward a reinforcement of colonial social structures? Or would it be a bold and uncertain transformation into something new? And if the latter, by political reform or revolution? This reality was one sign of the times, and Romero keenly felt the call to read it in the light of the Gospel. His third pastoral letter, co-published with Bishop Rivera y Damas of Santiago de María on August 6, 1978, did exactly that. Sadly, this moment further solidified and revealed the divisions among the bishops. The other four bishops hastily wrote an opposing letter and published it under the authority of the Salvadoran bishops' conference.

Romero's pastoral letter presented a profound theology of the Church's relationship to politics and popular organizations. There, he insisted that the Church cannot remain distanced from the rightful longings of the people for a more just society. Many of those in the popular organizations were inspired by their Christian faith and their reading of the Bible to demand a more just society. And further, regardless of this Christian inspiration, Romero noted that the teachings of the Church clearly support the right to organize to seek political and economic reform. He condemned the violent repression carried out by the government and military. But he also tried to guide his people through the messiness of relating Christian faith to politics.

Faith and politics, he said, should be "unified but not identified." Unified, because one should lead an integrated life in which one's faith infuses every commitment—including the political. If I confess the dignity of every person as a son or daughter of God on Sunday, this confession should obviously impact every dimension of my life, from my prayers, to my family life, to my political vision. It makes sense when the Gospel inspires the hungry and landless *campesino* to join in the struggle for a more just society. Romero praises such maturity of faith and defends the right of all to organize and demand change. However, Romero warned many times of the temptation to put one's total faith, trust, and allegiance in a particular organization. In fact, even good popular organizations can become idols. He wrote,

> Political activity tends to absorb, indeed to monopolize, a person's interest. This is a perfectly normal phenomenon of human enthusiasm. However, there arises at times a tension between two loyalties, loyalty to the faith and loyalty to the organization... the final and definitive loyalty of a Christian

can never be to a human organization, no matter what advantages it may offer, but to God and to the poor, who are the 'least of the brethren' of Jesus Christ.[1]

On September 10, 1978, Romero's homily turned again to these subjects. He opens by reiterating the core themes of his third pastoral letter. He then presents the central theme of the homily: "The Church: A Prophetic Community, a Sacramental Community, and a Community of Love." This homily takes up and develops further many of the themes we have already seen in this book, and it offers a clear vision of the prophetic task of the whole Christian community. In one of the most famous moments of all Romero's preaching, he insists: "The prophetic mission, therefore, is a duty of God's people. That's why, when some people scornfully say that I think I'm a prophet, I respond, 'God be praised! You also must become one! Every Christian, the whole of God's people, every family must develop a prophetic sense. All of us must convey a sense of God's mission in the world; we must bring to it a divine presence that makes demands and also rejects!'" This was the path he offered to his people and the one that he himself took.

Suggestions for Further Reading

Thus far I have suggested additional homilies as further readings for those interested in engaging more deeply with

---

1. Óscar Romero, *Voice of the Voiceless: The Four Pastoral Letters and Other Statements*, trans. Michael J. Walsh (Orbis Books, 1985),101–102.

Romero's thought. As noted in my introduction to this homily, Romero's pastoral letters are another very important resource for encountering his vision of a prophetic Church. In particular, the second and third letters offer his more formal teaching as archbishop from 1977 and 1978.

- Second Pastoral Letter, "The Church, the Body of Christ in History" (August 6, 1977) in *Voice of the Voiceless: The Four Pastoral Letters and Other Statements,* trans. Michael J. Walsh (Orbis Books, 1985), 63–84.

- Third Pastoral Letter, "The Church and Popular Political Organizations" (August 6, 1978) in *Voice of the Voiceless,* 85–113.

Sunday, September 10, 1978
Mass Readings
Ezekiel 33:7–9; Romans 13:8–10
Matthew 18:15–20

Dear brothers and sisters, we have heard the biblical readings not only with human attentiveness but with true faith because it is the word of God. I am pleased to tell you that the readings coincide with the basic theological and pastoral approach of the pastoral letter that you are becoming familiar with these days.[1] I'm hoping that the pastoral letter becomes the object of study in the communities and that people reflect on it seriously. Unfortunately this week we couldn't produce as many copies as we had announced, but by the beginning of next week we'll have the new edition. Meanwhile, the complete text of the pastoral letter is being printed in the issue of *Orientación* that's available today. Whenever there is opportunity in your meetings or in your small groups or at home, please study the letter, and you'll see that it's mainly concerned about the Church's identity, that is, the true nature and mission of the Church founded by Christ. This identity is based directly on the word of God that we'll be reflecting on today in light of the biblical texts. The nature and the mission of the Church is something that Catholics should have quite clear in their minds since they are the ones who form the Church. If we have a clear, precise, certain idea of what the Church is,

---

1. "The Church and the People's Political Organizations" (August 6, 1978).

we will then be able to help the world courageously with all its problems. That's what the Church is for; that's why Christ established it: not to preserve herself for the sake of preservation but to preserve herself to serve the world.

The theme of the pastoral letter is the relation of the Church to the people's organizations. The Church must provide a service to the organizations of *campesinos*, workers, politicians, and all those who want to organize for the sake of a better nation and a better world. The Church would be at fault if she just drew apart with the treasures of her doctrine and her moral force and failed to respond to the anguished questions of the modern world and our own nation with counsels based on God's word, counsels that only she can give. We have repeated often that the Church is not a people's organization, but in our pastoral letter we insist that the Church, without identifying with such organizations, provides them an invaluable service. We explain this in the pastoral letter as follows.

First, it is precisely in community that many Christians have become aware of how the Gospel and Christian justice demand that we help to transform this unjust world. Consequently, the Church is not ashamed that people have emerged from their communities with definite political and social concerns. The Council itself reminds us that one of the most serious needs at the present time is civic and political education and that persons skilled in this noble art of politics should receive preparation and training (*Gaudium et Spes* 75). So the Church is not ashamed that reflection on the word of God has produced many political activists and many organized groups. Nevertheless, the Church remains true to herself; she is like the mother at home who lets go of her children once she has educated them. She rejoices in her knowledge that she has given them a critical awareness and a sense of responsibility as they go out into the world to seek concrete situations for which they can take responsibility.

On the basis of her identity and without confusing herself with the organizations, the Church defends the right of people to organize. This is a human right. No one can prohibit people from organizing with others as long as the objectives they seek are honest and good—to survive, to have food for their families, to improve their living conditions. The Church defends—and has defended, thank God—this right of organization.

Another vital service of the Church, one we defend in the pastoral letter, is supporting the just demands that any organization might promote. It's not necessary for the organization to be Christian. As long as an organization is seeking a just objective, the Church supports it, because her duty is to defend the justice of the kingdom of God. Whenever there is some reflection of God's kingdom in any human group, the Church knows that God is present there and asks us to commit ourselves to defending the justice being sought.

There is still another service the Church provides. Since her singular strength is the Gospel and nothing else, the Church has the Gospel-given duty and right to denounce whatever is found to be unjust, evil, or sinful in any organization, even in one called Christian. The Church is not so committed to any one organization that she cannot say, "That is wrong! This is sinful! That I must denounce! This I repudiate!'" And thank God, the Church has done this. Here in the archdiocese the Church's duty has been to defend what is just and condemn what is unjust.

Another important service the Church provides is to take the concerns of those who are seeking justice and defending their temporal rights and to incorporate them into Christ's great liberation, his grand redemption. In order to do this the

Church tells every person and every organization seeking just and noble ends, "That's good, but it's not enough. Integrate it into Christian redemption. You need to be freed from sin, for Christ came to break the chains of sin. Your liberation will not be complete unless you develop more and become a child of God by grace and holiness; it will not be complete if you prescind from Christ and trust only in earthly ideologies. I want to serve you, to lead you by the hand toward true redemption, for that is your true destiny, the ultimate vocation of all men and women." This is the great service of the Church. But in order to provide this service and establish relations with earthly organizations and human groups, the Church must be in full possession of herself; she must be sure of her identity as Church. This is the comparison Paul VI used in his first encyclical *Ecclesiam Suam*: when a doctor goes to a disease-infested area, she immunizes herself in order to stay well; otherwise she'd end up sick herself. For what use is a sick doctor to sick people? That's why the Church has to go forth immunized with her own identity. The Church cannot let herself be confused with any earthly organization or ideology if she is to render her true service as Church for their benefit, just as a doctor provides her true service of healing sick people by immunizing herself so as not to become sick. I'm not saying that all the organizations are sick, but I'm making the comparison to show you that the Church in rendering these services must first of all define clearly the nature of her mission, and that's what we do in our pastoral letter.

I don't want to go too long, so I won't read to you pages 20 and 21 of the letter—you're going to study it yourselves. There, taking words from the Church's teaching, the letter says that if there is a group of people who believe in Christ, accept his teaching, and manifest this by belonging to his Church through baptism, then those people will nourish their

Christian life with God's word and will manifest their encounter with Christ by the sacramental signs: confession and communion (*Evangelii Nunciandi* 13; 23). That's what Church is! Church is a group of people who are nourished by the word of God and by the Eucharist just as you are being nourished today in coming to Mass. This is what the Church is!

Here we are in the church this Sunday, sisters and brothers, and those who have listened to me with sincerity, without prejudice, without hatred, without ill will, without trying to defend indefensible interests—such persons cannot say I am preaching political sermons or subversive sermons. All that is calumny, nothing more. You are listening to me at this moment, and what I'm saying is what I've always said. What I want to state here in the cathedral pulpit is what the Church is. What I want to say is that the Church supports, applauds, and encourages whatever is good; she consoles the victims of assaults and injustice; and she also denounces the atrocities, the disappearances, the tortures, and the social injustice. That is not meddling in politics. That is building up the Church and fulfilling the duty the Church has by her very identity. My conscience is quite tranquil, and I call on all of you to help us build up the true Church! For this task we are given help by the word that has been read today.

The Gospel of Saint Matthew gives us the principal readings for the whole of this year, so let us pay attention to his thought. Sunday after Sunday we've been reading short passages from the Gospel of Saint Matthew, and in order to understand them better we also take a passage from the Old Testament which illuminates the Gospel. Today the text from Ezekiel sheds marvelous light on the problem Jesus Christ is dealing with in the Gospel of Saint Matthew. Also, the letters of the apostles are like direct deductions from Christ's teachings.

What we see, then, is that the Gospel, seen in the light of the Old Testament and commented on in the letters of the apostles, communicates to us that this Church of the Archdiocese of San Salvador in 1978 is the same Church that Christ announced in his Gospel; it is the same Church that the prophets announced and that the apostles taught to the first Christians. This is the great honor I feel, sisters and brothers, and that's why I am happy that there is an overall positive reaction to my preaching and that my words are heard with the sincere desire to know and to build the true Church of Christ here among us, in El Salvador in 1978.

I told you that I had an outline of the Gospel of Saint Matthew, and I'm quite delighted to know that many people, on hearing this, are asking for copies. This is good, since Matthew supplies the readings for this year. Do not expect a book; it's just an outline, a couple of pages. It's already there in the Jerusalem Bible for those of you who have that version. At the beginning of the Gospels there is the heading: "Introduction to the Synoptic Gospels." Look for the Gospel of Matthew there, and you'll find the precious commentary that says that the Gospel of Saint Matthew is like a drama about the coming of God's kingdom in seven acts. It describes the Gospel and indicates the chapters that correspond to each act of this extraordinary drama. In its fifth act, which is chapters 16 to 18, the Gospel speaks about the beginning of God's kingdom on earth in terms of a group of disciples with Peter at their head. The norms of life for this newborn Church are sketched out in the community discourse. Today's passage is taken precisely from chapter 18, which is part of Christ's discourse about community.

Remember that the Gospels are not so much a biography of Christ as they are the reflections of the first communities on Christ's teachings. As a fruit of those reflections, the apostles wrote down the discourses of Christ that they remembered, but this was only after the community had reflected on them. It's wonderful to know, then, that this chapter 18 is the fruit of the first Christian community; it tells us what that newly created Church was like as it burst forth from its source in Christ.

This reading speaks of the humility that all pastors should have. The apostles argued about which of them was the greatest—the same hierarchical quarrels as always. Christ tells them, "No, here those who wish to be great should become like children and servants of all" (Matt 18:1–5). Authority in the Church is not commanding; it is serving. In Christianity, those who do not become like simple children cannot enter the kingdom of heaven. What shame I feel as pastor—and I ask my community for forgiveness—when I have not been able to fulfill my role as bishop by serving you! I am not the boss; I am not the one in charge; I am not an authority that imposes itself. I want to be God's servant and yours.

In speaking about what community should be like, Christ is calling us to be authentic, and so from today's three readings I can draw the title of my homily: "The Church: a Prophetic Community, a Sacramental Community, and a Community of Love." That's what the Church is!

If we don't understand it that way, then we don't know what the Church of Christ is. These three characteristics serve as a summary of today's three readings.

The Church Is a Prophetic Community

First of all, I want to tell you that the Church that Christ wanted is a prophetic community. Commenting on this idea, the Council stated in *Lumen Gentium*, section 12, "The holy people of God shares also in Christ's prophetic office; it spreads abroad a living witness to him, especially by means of a life of faith and charity" (*Lumen Gentium* 12). So you see that all of you, sisters and brothers, are the prophetic people, a people that God has organized to spread abroad a living witness of his teaching. The same Council, in speaking about married persons, that is, you lay people, says that matrimony and family life provide a propitious setting for developing this prophetic sense of the people of God. When parents live holy lives in close contact with their children, they are like a small Church; by their virtues they encourage society to be holy, and they also reproach whatever is evil, unjust and sinful in the world (*Lumen Gentium* 11). There is no greater reproach for a sinful society than a holy family. And so the people of God and the divine word deliver to all of us engaged in this reflection a solemn summons: as members of one family, let our homes and our relations as spouses and our relations as parents and children be models that bear witness to love, to holiness, to justice, and to charity in the midst of a world that is selfish, sinful, and violent. There is nothing more necessary in these times of violence and terrorism than holy homes that emanate love.

The prophetic mission, therefore, is a duty of God's people. That's why, when some people scornfully say that I think I'm a prophet, I respond, "God be praised! You also must become one! Every Christian, the whole of God's people, every family must develop a prophetic sense. All of us must convey a sense of God's mission in the world; we must bring to it a divine presence that makes demands and also rejects!" As Pope Paul VI said in his exhortation on evangelization in the modern world, let us suppose that a group of Christians proposes to live in an authentic way the Gospel in which they believe. This group just by itself stirs up great questions in the world: What kind of people are these? What are they hoping for? What do they love? Who are they? (*Evangelii Nunciandi* 21). That's the way Christianity began in Jerusalem. As we're told by the book of the Acts of the Apostles, the people kept joining the community because they saw how the Christians loved one another and praised God (Acts 2:47). It was a community with no social inequalities, a community where those who had something shared with those who had nothing, a community where no one was ashamed of being poor and nobody boasted of being rich. They bore witness to charity and love. A prophetic community announces simply by its presence what God expects of human beings in making them social creatures. I find all these thoughts, dear sisters and brothers, in today's readings.

The first reading is marvelous. It's said that few persons have entered so deeply into the mystery of God as the prophet Ezekiel—he almost seems abnormal. Do you realize that it's not shameful to be thought crazy? People thought the prophet Ezekiel was crazy, but the reason was that he had entered so deeply into God's world that ordinary people considered him abnormal. Who is really abnormal—those who have so distanced themselves from God that they think people seeking after God are abnormal, or those who attain normality in the very center of life that is God? Well, this prophet Ezekiel, who was crazy as far as the world was concerned, preached the great mystery you've heard today in the form of a parable.

Chapter 33 of Ezekiel is perhaps one of the most beautiful descriptions of the prophetic mission God wants to entrust to human beings. The parable goes as follows: When God allows a war to be waged against a nation, the people appoint a sentinel who watches out for the approaching enemy. When the enemy is near, the sentinel sounds a horn or a trumpet, as was the custom in those days, and the people in the city hear the trumpet. Those who hear the warning prepare to defend the city to save themselves, and of course the sentinel will also be saved, for he has done his duty. But if the people, after hearing the sentinel's warning, pay it no mind and end up being killed, the sentinel still is saved because he has done his job. On the other hand, says the parable, if the sentinel neglects his duty and fails to blow the trumpet, then the enemy will enter the city, and the defenders will not be able to defeat the enemy. In that case the sentinel is guilty of negligence, and if, because of his negligence, death comes upon those caught unawares in the city, then all are doomed, both sentinel and people. At this point the prophet applies the parable to his own mission, saying, "I am the sentinel." The prophet is a sentinel, a watchman, and when God says, "Be converted, you who do wrong!" the prophet must become God's trumpet and also declare, "Be converted, you who do wrong!" If the wrongdoers are not converted, they are lost, but the prophet has fulfilled his responsibility. If the prophet fails to cry out, the wrongdoers will be lost by their own fault, but God says, "I will also hold the prophet responsible because he did not cry out. He was not a trumpet. He was not a watchman" (Ezek 33:1–9).

We find this same parable in the Gospel, where Christ says, "If your brother commits an error, don't be remiss. Go and speak to him alone. If you correct him, you have won him for God. If he does not listen, call some witnesses who will testify to your diligence and to the obstinacy of the one who is wrong. If he does not listen to them either, then tell the community, tell the Church, and the Church will treat him as a Gentile and a tax collector" (Matt 18:15–17). In the language of Christ these two terms were used for persons who were excommunicated; because of their stubbornness they could no longer be part of the community.

Here, dear sisters and brothers, is where I find the explanation for why the Church has a prophetic mission. Why does a prophet have to intervene between God and the wrongdoers?

Why is the community called to give testimony in such a way that those who don't listen to the community are cast out? I find here two major explanations that I want you to pay close attention to.

The first explanation is how social sin can exist. Many are scandalized by this idea, saying that sin is personal but not social. Certainly that's what the Bible has told us today: "The wrongdoer will be lost by his own fault" (Ezek 33:8). But the text also mentions the co-responsibility of the prophet who makes no announcement. This applies to all of us who let injustices pass by, especially if they can be avoided. It applies to every family that panders to selfishness and fails to give a Christian meaning to life. It applies to every home that doesn't become as holy as God wants it to be but rather lives in sin. All of us have become contaminated with social sin; we have become accomplices in social sin. And when the situation, as is the case in El Salvador, becomes such that a law is decreed in order to preserve order, then we must ask, what order? The order is the order of injustice: "Don't disturb things. Let the situation remain as it is. Don't denounce anything because that is meddling in politics." El Salvador is living in what Medellín called a state of institutionalized sin.[2] Many thanks. Your response shows that we're in agreement:

---

2. CELAM, Medellín, "Peace," par. 16. The concept of "institutionalized sin" is addressed in the introduction to the next homily in this book.

the Church cannot be silent. We who are her pastors must speak out. We must all be a prophetic people and issue a warning call. But understand what the aim of this prophetic stance is. If you continue reading Ezekiel, in chapter 33 the prophet tells the children of Israel, his compatriots, "Don't be pessimistic! You have said, 'God has abandoned us because of our sins! Who can save us?'" The prophet then lifts up their spirits by declaring, "God also says, 'I do not want the death of sinners. I want them to be converted and to live. I am a God of forgiveness. I am a God who wants what is just. I am a God who, yes, makes demands and punishes but also a God who is ready to forgive'" (Ezek 33:10–11). At this point, sisters and brothers, I want to call upon the memory of all of you who have been kind enough to follow my thinking for more than a year now. Whenever there has been an assault, whenever we have condemned something, we have always ended with a call to conversion: "Let sinners be converted!" When we were celebrating here in the cathedral the funeral of Father Grande after he was murdered, we said, "I hope that we are being heard by those who killed him, and we call out to them in their murderers' den, 'Be converted for the Lord loves you and is waiting for you!'" There is never any hate, never any resentment in the prophet's denunciation. Neither can the prophetic people of God hate; they must love. The prophetic people, as today's gospel reading says, seeks out those who go wrong in order to win them over to God. The prophet, even as he speaks of the neglectful sentinel's punishment, also praises the mercy of the God who calls us. That's why I say to you, dear sisters and brothers, "Be converted!" I say this especially to you, my dear sisters and brothers who hate me; I say it to you, my dear sisters and brothers who think that I'm preaching violence and slander me even though you know it's not true;

I say it to you who have your hands stained with crime, torture, assault, injustice—I tell you all, "Be converted!" I love you dearly, and I feel sorry for you because you are traveling the paths of perdition.

The Church Is a Sacramental Community

My second thought is this: the Church is a sacramental community. In our pastoral letter we state that the Church has a great mission regarding earthly affairs, but she does not thereby lose herself in earthly things. If she did, the pope tells us, she would lose all her force (*Evangelii Nunciandi* 32). The Church would then not be announcing the true liberation of God, which involves the demands of the poor people asking for bread, the demands of the uneducated asking for learning, the demands of those who live in misery. The Church would then become miserable herself, incapable of inspiring people to hope for forgiveness and resurrection.

Indeed, the Church's mission is transcendent, for she can never forget the vision of God. And here precisely is the sign of community. I thank you, dear communities, those I've had the good fortune to visit and those I haven't been able to visit but I know are alive. This week I received some very delightful letters from Christian communities that have placed their trust in this word of God; they come not only from the archdiocese but from other dioceses. I thank you profoundly, and I tell you: Keep your hope strong. Preserve this sacramental sign of the Church. Be communities that struggle for just claims, but never forget that the only one who can give us strength and inspiration is God.

In this regard, today's gospel gives us some insight. What does Christ say there? "Where two or three are gathered together in my name, there am I in the midst of them"

(Matt 18:20). Thank you, Lord, because wherever there is a community that sits down and reflects on your word with religious sincerity, there you become present, blessed Christ, Liberator of humankind. How can my heart not be filled with hope by a Church in which base communities of faith flourish! And why should I not ask my dear fellow priests to help these communities to flourish everywhere—in the neighborhoods, in the villages, among families? "Because wherever two or three are gathered in my name," there is the sacramental sign (Matt 18:20).

Here in the cathedral Christ is now present. The protagonist here this morning is Christ our Lord. He is bearing witness to us that Christ is present not only in the consecrated host, but in all of us who form one community. Christ is present in every group of Christians gathered around a radio and meditating on this word of God. Here is Christ! Blessed be God that we aren't going it alone!

Thus we can see that the Church community is sacramental. What is a sacrament? It is a visible sign of an invisible reality. What is visible are your faces, many known to one another from the cordial greetings we exchange as we leave. All this is the visible community. But what is invisible is the face we don't see but believe in, and we discover it through the faces of one another. It is Christ our Lord.

There is another reality in this sacramental community. Christ tells us, "When two of you agree in asking something of my Father, my Father in heaven will grant it to you" (Matt 18:19). What a beautiful thing! The community is a sign of God's will because God grants only what is asked for according to his will, and God's will as reflected in community is very different from what many people would like to think is God's will. Many people would like poor people to keep on saying, "It's God's will that I live this way." But it is not the will of God that some people have everything while others have nothing. That cannot be of God. God's will is that all his children should be happy. When two or three agree in asking something of God, God grants it. That is the community of love, the will that unites in God. How marvelous it is to know that this morning also our prayer and our Mass will be heard by God because there are more than two of us! The cathedral is full, and so, united with Christ, we can ask the Father for what our society needs. Let us therefore make our Sunday Mass, as I said at the beginning, a time of hope.

In the third place there is the presence of God who accepts or rejects. "If after you speak to the sinner, either alone or with witnesses, he pays you no mind, then tell the community; and if he pays no heed to the community, let him be excommunicated and set apart" (Matt 18:15–17). This is where Christ uses the words he spoke to Peter, "Whatever you bind on earth shall be bound in heaven, and whatever you loose on earth, shall be loosed in heaven" (Matt 18:18). Pay close attention to this, dear sisters and brothers: what was given as a prerogative of the pope is not something exclusive to the pope; it is something God gives to the whole people of God, even if the pope is the supreme expression of this privilege. Christ told Peter in an exclusive sense, "Whatever you bind on earth, shall be bound in heaven" (Matt 16:19), and now he tells the community: "Whatever you in union with your pastors consider to be error, is error." The infallible judgment will be pronounced by the pope, but the whole people of God also enjoys these prerogatives when they are in communion—in community—with their pastors. This must be kept very much in mind so that we realize that in each diocese the bishop in communion with the pope is the sign of this unity and truth.

The Church Is a Community of Love

Finally, dear sisters and brothers, let us say a word about today's second reading, which speaks about the Church community as a community of love. The Council expresses it beautifully when it speaks about the characteristics of the people of God: "That messianic people has Christ the Redeemer for its head. . . . The state of this people is that of the dignity and freedom of the children of God, in whose hearts the Holy Spirit dwells as in his temple. Its law is the new commandment to love as Christ loved us. Its end is the kingdom of God, which has been begun by God himself on earth" (*Lumen Gentium* 9). It would be hard to find more beautiful words. The identity of our Church should be characterized by love. In El Salvador we say that the Constitution should be respected because it is the soul of nationhood. The constitution of Christians is a single word: love.

That's why Saint Paul says, "The one who loves his neighbor has fulfilled the law because the commandments, 'You shall not steal,' 'You shall not kill,' "You shall not harm another,'are all summed up in a single word: 'You shall love your neighbor'" (Rom 13:8–9). If there existed true love of neighbor, there would be no terrorism, no repression, no selfishness, no cruel inequalities in our society, no abductions, and no crimes. Love is the synthesis of the law, but not just the synthesis; it is what gives a Christian sense to all human relations. That's why even those who are called atheists, if they are humane, are fulfilling the essence of the relations that God wants among human beings: love. Love is the fullness of all human obligations, and without love, justice is only the sword. With love, however, justice becomes a fraternal embrace. Without love, laws are arduous, repressive, cruel, controlling; but where there is love, security forces are superfluous; where there is love, there are no jails, no torture, no will to beat people down.

This is what the Church is, dear sisters and brothers, and our job is to build this prophetic community, this sacramental community, this community of love. That is the essence of my preaching. But my preaching would be pure theory if we didn't look hard at the world outside the Church and examine it precisely from the perspective of the reality and inner life of our Church. We must understand the situation within which the Church's mission must be carried out in order to see if we are truly building our prophetic Church, our sacramental Church, our Church of love.

> *[Romero's homily continued as usual with sections on the "Life of the Church" and the "Events of the Week." What follows is just one paragraph from the latter and then the final paragraph of the homily as a whole.]*

Because of what's happening in Nicaragua, people are talking about the communist threat, which I admit we cannot ignore, but I would also remind you, dear sisters and brothers, that we are certainly not Marxists. We are anti-Marxists by reason of our Gospel principles, but we want to remind you also that the real struggle against Marxism consists in eliminating the causes that engender Marxism. That means changing the breeding ground in which it develops and offering an alternative to take its place. It's easy to cry out against Marxism and point to its influence everywhere—and certainly the danger in Nicaragua is great—but I also tell you, sisters and brothers, that "this mud comes from that dust!" We possibly still have time to apply medicine to the root of the problem: the best anti-Marxism is a more just society that does away with the situations that give rise to Marxism.

. . .

Dear sisters and brothers, it is not for reasons of scandal or spectacle that the prophetic Church must expose the social conditions where she is working; rather, she does so because it is her duty. She does so because if the prophet fails to cry out, "Be converted, you who do wrong!" the wrongdoers may perish, but the prophet will also perish for not speaking their prophetic word. And now, so that the Lord Jesus Christ, the eternal Prophet, will give us the strength we need to live as a Church ever more inserted into the present reality as a truly sacramental community of our people, as a community that prophesies about these realities, and above all as a community of love that binds us together in the Lord, let us celebrate the Eucharist. That is where we find the nourishment of this community that is not to be confused with other organizations but that serves all organizations by preserving its own identity as prophetic, sacramental, and loving! Let it be so.

The Voice of Blood

(June 21, 1979)

A true prophetic word is always a word of love. As we read in the previous homily: "There is never any hate, never any resentment in the prophet's denunciation. Neither can the prophetic people of God hate; they must love. The prophetic people, as today's gospel says, seeks out those who go wrong in order to win them over to God." The prophet has a hard calling. Sin must be named. Oppression must be condemned. The lives of the innocent must be defended. Yet somehow the prophet must keep at bay the pull toward vengeance, retribution, and hatred. In the short term, each of these can offer a powerful impulse for gathering people to fight for change. But they ultimately explode into uncontrollable cycles of violence and will consume the person from within.

The true prophet ultimately aims to build something positive. One thinks here of Martin Luther King, Jr.'s longing for the "beloved community." The prophet longs for a society in which all can truly flourish. The suffering of the poor and oppressed is a cry to the heavens that the prophet must respond to; the prophet longs for society which will "let justice roll down like waters and righteousness like an ever-flowing stream" (Amos 5:24). However, it is crucial that the prophet desire the flourishing of the oppressor as well. In a different way, certainly. Nevertheless, a life centered on wealth and dependent on the suffering of one's neighbor is not the "more abundant" life that Jesus promised (John 10:10). This is what makes the prophet's call to conversion an act of love.

The prophet speaks in the hope that *all* will respond to the call to contribute to the great project of God's kingdom. The true prophet is no demagogue. The demagogue has their constituency and can simply condemn the rest. For the true prophet, even the harshest, most uncompromising condemnation is for the sake of healing, transformation, and a building up. Romero's appeal to a medical metaphor in his preaching is instructive here. The prophet tells society where it is sick *so that it can receive treatment*. The prophet points to an open wound, *so that it can receive attention and healing*. All of this is to be an act of love.

Yet Romero wasn't naïve about how society responds to the prophet. As we read earlier, "No one wants to have a sore spot touched, and therefore a society with so many sores reacts strongly when someone has the courage to touch the sore and say, 'You have to treat that.'" Some people will truly hear the words of the prophet and be converted. Romero's own transformation is a great example of this. However, whether in the Bible or in Romero's time, more often the prophet is rejected and persecuted. Thus, the prophetic Church is also the persecuted Church.

By the summer of 1979, the persecution of the people and the Church had reached levels that Romero could not have imagined earlier—and would only continue to worsen as his own death approached. Those listening to Romero's homilies would have heard a litany of suffering:

the persecution of catechists, the targeting of teachers, the indiscriminate attacks on the rural poor, and, increasingly, the phenomenon of "disappearances." Romero named this suffering and persecution in detail:

June 3, 1979: "There were also fifty-five persons arrested this month, and thirty of them are now listed among the disappeared. This is a sad reality in our country. The mother of one disappeared person has a serious heart problem, and yet she finds no response to her question: "Where is my son?""

June 10: "How can the God of our people not be on the side of the fourteen teachers who have been murdered since April 24? During this month dedicated to teachers we remember the names of these dead teachers: Noel Saúl Ramos, Ricardo Villalobos, Emma Guadalupe Carpio, Rafael Vázquez Marín, Antonio Merino, René Mauricio Pacheco, Orlando Guerrero Chamul, Pedro Federico Colorado, Francisco Borja Carranza, René Guevara, Lázaro Arias, José Manuel Funes Minero, Manuel de Jesús Chávez, Héctor Joaquín Torres. Fourteen mentors of our children, killed!"

June 17: Let us now look at the wave of violence that continues to spread, especially among teachers. Twenty-two have been killed already; two have disappeared, Juan José Herrera and Roberto Romero; two have been seriously wounded; and many threats have been received from the [White Warrior Union]. I recall with emotion what a teacher in a small town told his students: "I'm leaving you because I've received a death threat, and I don't know if I'll be able to teach you again." Many schools in the country have been closed because of threats and fear.... There are more victims of the violence. ... The *campesinos* Manuel Barahona Chávez, Domingo Murcia, and Rubén Quezada were arrested and then found shot to death. Three other unidentified bodies were found in Tierra Blanca.... Yesterday they also threatened a priest,[1] and in recent days they've threatened several other Christians. Regarding kidnapping, we continue to be concerned about the two Englishmen. We also mention and request your concern for three other kidnap victims: Adolfo Antonio Rios, Miguel Armando Miguel, and Carlos Rafael Nieto Álvarez.

Among these victims were many priests, religious, and catechists. But not all priests, for example, were targeted. Rather, those who remained present to their communities and committed to their liberation were the ones slandered, threatened, and attacked.

Father Rafael Palacios was one of those deeply committed priests, and, on June 20, 1979, he became the fifth priest killed during Romero's time as archbishop. Romero saw his death as a great tragedy but also as a sign of the faithfulness of the Church: "In a country where so many people are being murdered so horribly, it would be sad if we found no priests also among the victims. They are the testimony of a Church incarnated in the problems of her people." Father Palacios was one of those priests in solidarity with the people, both in life and in death. A Mass on his behalf, Romero

---

1. Father Rafael Palacios.

says, should remind all not only "of the five murdered priests, but it is also our people's earnest entreaty on behalf of the blood of all our sacrificed sisters and brothers, Christian and non-Christian alike. Life is always sacred" (June 30, 1979).

At the funeral Mass on June 21, Romero let his homily echo the witness of Father Palacios: "Dear sisters and brothers, the voice of blood speaks the most eloquent language of all. That is why this *cathedra* feels strengthened by the testimony of blood that has now become an oft-heard voice in this cathedral. Here has been spilled the blood of the people and the blood of priests." Romero details in his homily the vicious cycle of sin and violence that was enveloping the country. In order to understand this vicious cycle, Romero will turn as he often does to Church teaching and the language of Catholic social doctrine. In particular, he draws upon the ideas of the episcopal conference at Medellín to speak of a "structure of sin" and a "structure of violence." Elsewhere he calls these "institutionalized sin" or "institutionalized violence," concepts that are crucial for understanding his diagnosis of Salvadoran reality.

Long histories of sin, oppression, and discrimination give rise to social structures that dominate societies. These structures can be political, in an unjust restriction of the right to vote. They can be economic, as when a small minority hoards immense wealth while the majority suffers; and they can be cultural, as when certain groups are viewed and treated as less than human. Each of these originates and is supported by the acts of individuals, but they become a sort of collective structure that defines society.

These sinful or violent structures operate in at least three ways: first, they create great suffering. Sin always brings death. Romero saw this all around him. The *campesinos* working the large plantations endured so much suffering and many died far too young. They worked long hours in the heat, yet did not have their own land, a just wage, access to education, or even basic healthcare. The suffering of the poor is a sign of the sin of society. Second, such structures deform our conscience and worldview. A child raised in a culture that makes money the god above all else is likely to do the same. The child of a plantation owner is likely to feel entitled to the wealth and power that comes with such land and to be indifferent to the suffering all around them. Third, such structures often mask the reality of their violence; indeed, often they create something that looks like peace. The large plantation owners did not see themselves as violently oppressing their workers. Most of them did not actually steal land to create their grand estates; that happened at least a half-century earlier and often through legal—though exploitative—maneuvers. Walking out in the cool morning and surveying the hundreds of workers picking coffee beans, "peace" would probably feel like the right word. Yet, this would be ignoring the violence inscribed in the deepest marrow of the society.

For Romero, the prophet cannot ignore such structures, for the root problem must be addressed if society is truly to move forward toward the common good. A few more tortillas and a small literacy program are not an adequate response. Furthermore, at some point, the suffering caused by institutionalized violence will give rise to demands for change. And here is the specter of that cycle of violence which spirals out of control. In Romero's day, the oligarchy saw reform movements as a powerful threat to their place in the country and responded with repressive violence. Thus, the silent institutionalized violence, already supported by legal structures and policing tactics, transforms into explicit repressive violence in the face of movements for change. In the US context, one only has to recall images of dogs and fire hoses unleashed on peaceful protesters in the Civil Rights Movement.

But the cycle does not stop there. The longing for justice is not so easily suppressed. Repressive violence is likely to radicalize at least some portion of the movement for reform. At this point, acts of terrorism and calls for revolution emerge, both of which will become a further excuse for a dramatic increase in repressive violence. In Romero's El Salvador, this took the particularly vicious form of the military employing a vast network of right-wing death squads funded by the oligarchy. Romero insisted that we must see and reject every part of this cycle of violence, but also that it would continue as long as the structural causes are not addressed. This was the point of Romero's remark about fighting Marxism in a previous homily: "the real struggle against Marxism consists in eliminating the causes that engender Marxism."

Romero was also clear about what the prophet should expect: when the prophet touches this social wound and names it for what it is, the patient will often recoil from the pain. The prophet is defamed, slandered, and persecuted—even to the point of death. For Romero, Father Rafael Palacios was one of these prophets who dared to speak, who dared to illuminate the reality of the country with the light of the Gospel. At his funeral, Romero sought to hear his voice, to hear his witness to the Church and the country, now given in the voice of blood.

Suggestions for Further Reading

After this homily, Romero preached two more times on the witness of Father Rafael Palacios and the tragic state of the country. First, Romero again celebrated a "Single Mass," in which he canceled all liturgies in the archdiocese in order to gather as one. Second, Romero took up the prophetic call to announce the Gospel and denounce sin at a memorial Mass a month after Palacio's death.

- "The Single Mass" (June 30, 1979) in *A Prophetic Bishop Speaks to His People: The Complete Homilies of Archbishop Óscar Arnulfo Romero*, 6 vols., trans. Joseph Owens, SJ (Convivium Press, 2015–2016), 5.66–72.

- "Why Did They Kill Rafael Palacios?" (July 20, 1979) in *A Prophetic Bishop Speaks*, 5.131–36.

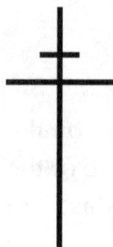

Esteemed Bishop Rivera of Santiago de María and dear fellow priests of this archdiocese and our sister dioceses, I thank you for sharing this time of pain with us.

Dear sisters and brothers, the voice of blood speaks the most eloquent language of all. That is why this *cathedra* feels strengthened by the testimony of blood that has now become an oft-heard voice in this cathedral. Here has been spilled the blood of the people and the blood of priests. In this cathedral we have tried to interpret the language of all the blood that has been shed around our country: in the mountains, on the highways, on the beaches, in the streets of our cities. What place has not already been flooded with the blood which this cathedral, as interpreter of this language of pain and anguish, has tried to make into a message of consolation and hope?

Today in the cathedral it is the blood of a priest that is crying out. Rafael Palacios gave his life not only yesterday, when he was gunned down in a street of Santa Tecla, but he gave it from the moment his life began and was dedicated to God. There in the village of Talcualuya in San Luis Talpa, in the department of La Paz, he was born of Don Rafael and Doña Concepción on October 16, 1938. The mutual love of child and parents remained always strong, inspiring Rafael with a sense of family and guaranteeing that he would always tread the path of goodness. They moved to Suchitoto, which became the adoptive town of Rafael and his brothers and sisters, who are here present. He served as priest in the parish of Tecoluca and in the cathedral of the diocese of San Vicente. Later he ministered in this archdiocese, first in Santa Tecla and Ilopango and most recently in the parish of San Francisco in Mejicanos.

This long trajectory of Rafael Palacios tells us that his was a life characterized by integrity, love of study, and pursuit of the truth, perhaps almost to excess. For that is what made him the victim that we accept here today, the fifth priest killed in our diocese.[1] We hold him with the same respect and love with which we have held the other priests and with which we have bowed before so many other cruel deaths, which are now uncountable. We are celebrating here now with great solemnity not only because he was a priest—whose murder seems inconceivable in a people that claims to be Christian—but because his blood cries out from the depths and invites us all to listen intently this morning to this message of blood, which I think is expressed in three ideas: it is a revelation of the mystery of iniquity; it is a revelation of the mystery of fidelity to Jesus; and it is a message of hope for our people.

A Revelation of the Mystery of Iniquity

More than anything, I hear in the murder of Father Rafael the voice of his blood denouncing the iniquity of our people, which is sin. The most logical and eloquent manifestation of

---

1. The other priests killed were Rutilio Grande, March 12, 1977; Alfonso Navarro, May 11, 1977; Ernesto Barrera, November 28, 1978; and Octavio Ortiz, January 20, 1979.

sin is death—"by sin death entered the world", says the Bible (Rom 5:12). But when death results directly from sin, then it is due to criminal disobedience of the fifth commandment, "You shall not kill" (Exod 20:13), and we see clearly how sin and death are the mystery of iniquity.

In the silence of death Father Rafael denounces the sin of the world, but with respect I say that he also denounces the sin of the Church, and in all sincerity I say that he also denounces his own personal sin.

The sin of the world, first of all. Like Christ, the Church must continue to denounce the sin of the world. She must root out the sin of the world, even to the point of being crucified if necessary. We can say that the sin of the world is so evident in this death of Rafael that it puts on display the stupidity of violence and irrational vengeance. Why must the extreme right avenge the supposed sin of the extreme left by taking the life of a priest? These extremes constitute a sinful structure. Seeing the people of our country so polarized between right and left helps us to understand how serious the structural crisis in our nation is. There is a structure of sin and a structure of violence, as the bishops said in Medellín[2] and as long as that doesn't change, it will continue to reap victims, from both the left and the right.

It is irrational and stupid to take out on a priest what is supposedly the fault of the left. The priest belongs to neither the right nor the left. The priest has the loftiness of heart to love one and all. As a voice of the Church, the priest is love, and if by preferential option he takes the side of the poor, he does so not to exclude those who have wealth but to tell them that they will not be saved until they feel as their own the anguish of the poor and take their side as ministers of the Lord.

---

2. CELAM, Medellín, "Peace," pars. 1, 2, and 16.

They will be happy not by selfishly holding on to their wealth but by sharing it with everyone, just as God shares his.

It is wrong to kill a priest so criminally, so treacherously, so deliberately. On Saturday night Father Rafael came to look for me; he gave me a letter telling about the threats made against him by the UGB [White Warrior Union] on Thursday. On his little car they had painted their fateful hand of vengeance. Yesterday, or rather the day before, Father Palacios was with me at a vicariate meeting in his parish in Mejicanos. At the end he said to me, "Today they killed a soldier and I've been threatened. Something serious is going to happen in Santa Tecla." He sensed the danger, and so it was. I thought he was exaggerating, but yesterday I was shocked by the tragic news. I thought: how dire is the situation of our native land!

If it's true that the death of Father Palacios was a vendetta for the soldier's death the day before—the same was said about the death of Father Navarro, which was supposed to avenge the kidnapping and murder of the day before—then what basis is there for these acts of vengeance? For that reason I believe that our denunciation of the death of Father Rafael constitutes a demand for justice. Those who have in their hands the power to control these hellish, murderous forces must control them. When they want to do so, they can. I remember when the same phantom organization was threatening the Jesuit Fathers; the president of the republic made a plea for sanity and the threats stopped. So action is possible when there is a desire to take action.

How long will we put up with these crimes without justice being done? Where is the justice of our nation? Where is the Supreme Court of Justice? Where is the honor of our democracy if people must die this way, like dogs, without even investigating deaths like that of Father Rafael? In the name of the citizenry I ask and demand that investigations be carried out and that this growing spiral of violence be halted, since at least one of the groups is controlled by persons who can rein them in.

This structural sin has infested our society so thoroughly that we have become almost insensitive to it. It is incredible to think that our fear of a possible communist threat has made us forget about the awful sin that is already a reality in our midst. At this moment when we have before us yet another victim of these unjust structures, we must reflect on the urgent need to organize the life of our country in a different way. The powerful classes that control the government of the country need to evaluate these forces that have been made so violent by repression. Why has no sanction been placed as well on the forces of the right, which are also stupid and violent?

Poor Father Palacios! You have paid the price that logically awaited you in your ministry of revealing and denouncing the situation of our country. Rafael knew our reality, and he studied it in the light of the Gospel, which cannot fail to throw light on the injustices, the disorders, and the violence. Doing that naturally incites the arrogant hands of those who are sinning but don't want to be told that they are sinning.

That is why I also say, with great respect and humility, that the death of Father Rafael denounces the sins of the Church. Pardon me, sisters and brothers, but we are all Church, and when family members gather before a corpse, they must say honestly, "Maybe we are partly to blame." Let us accept our guilt. Sin is a sad inheritance of a Church that is composed of human beings. Although by grace she is continually tending toward conversion, there are many people who don't allow themselves to be carried by this current of conversion. What happens, then, is that the priest who is faithfully trying to denounce an unjust situation in the world perhaps gets no support from his pastors or his fellow priests or the people of God themselves. It's possible, sisters and brothers, that we have in some way collaborated with the unjust accusations that make the priest a man sentenced to death.

I think that Father Rafael's death should make us reflect and react. We should study what is being preached and try to understand how the Church is being renewed. Instead of installing ourselves in a cozy corner that resists any evolution in the life of the Church, we should have the courage to follow those who strive to keep up with the voice of the Church. We should not condemn or malign their voices, nor should we doubt them. Love and fraternal correction come first. Condemnation done with love is necessary for us, even within the Church, but we should never help our enemies by putting in their hands the weapons they will later use to do away with the dear members of our Church.

This is the time to reflect on the sins of the Church, which we all commit. And the person who denounces must also be willing to be denounced. I am saying this with Christian and evangelical bluntness to all the faithful, beginning with myself: we must analyze our conduct with regard to the demands of a Church that cannot renege on her preferential commitment to the poor, on her denunciation of sin, and on everything else that makes her a follower of our Lord Jesus Christ.

That's why I also say that the voice of Father Rafael's blood has called us together at this moment to celebrate this Eucharist and to ask for mercy for him and for his own sin. What priest does not feel that he is a sinner? At the moment of offering the sacrifice, he is the first to remind the people, "I confess before God that I am a sinner, and I ask you to pray for me."

This moment of sincerity at the hour of death is not the time for us to throw veils of hypocrisy over the sins, the defects, or the weaknesses of the deceased. Any one of us could point out defects in Father Palacios, but now is the time to say, "Father, forgive him because he also needs your mercy and your forgiveness."

In this way, then, his blood in all sincerity cries out against sin wherever it may be found.

A Revelation of the Mystery of Fidelity to Jesus

My second point is that this voice of the blood shed by Father Rafael reveals to us the mystery of fidelity. There is no fidelity without blood. God himself used blood to sign his covenant of fidelity with humankind. We were reminded of this last Sunday in the first reading, which spoke of the blood sprinkled on the altar and on the people (Exod 24:3–8). True communion cannot be manifested or expressed without blood. That's why I believe Christ, the model for Christians, had to seal his fidelity to our God with blood. And all those who wish to be faithful followers of Christ and of God must also authenticate their following under the seal of blood.

This is the great testimony that Rafael Palacios is giving us this morning: he was faithful to his vocation to the point of being gunned down for fulfilling his priestly duty. His fidelity to the Church is something I have often witnessed: it was a fidelity inspired in the Gospel and from the Gospel, a fidelity bold enough to denounce the very sins of the Church. What is important is that the Church be faithful to Jesus Christ, and in the Church the voice of those who want to be faithful to Jesus Christ will often have something important to say to other members of the Church.

There was his fidelity to the poor. Rafael was poor. He was always clean and well-groomed and carried himself with dignity, but he was poor. I can say that with all sincerity. His fidelity to poverty led him to be a priest without attachment to money. He used to celebrate Mass and serve the people in other ways without concern for stipends or what people might pay him. Priestly ministry is truly prostituted when it becomes a business! Fidelity to poverty is admirable when priestly ministry is guided by it, for then the poor priest can speak also to the wealthy, since the best testimony is the experience of living poverty.

A Message of Hope for Our People

Finally, dear sisters and brothers, from this hour of the Church's suffering I want us to gather a message of hope. When a Christian or a priest is killed, certainly we feel grief. We have heard the deep wailing and seen the tears of the communities that knew Father Rafael, and I have been moved by it. "If he sowed love, why did they kill him?" asked one of his faithful yesterday. But we should not weep without hope. I believe that the people's grieving shows that Rafael's testimony, which leaves behind a firm imprint of the Gospel of love, will be for us the seed of even more fruitful evangelization.

So I believe that the priestly witness of Rafael, sealed with the shedding of his blood, is truly a reason for hope. In him we behold the new man, and we feel the great desire he had to bring forth the new men and the new women so urgently needed today in Latin America to change not only structures but above all hearts.[3] (M 1,3). That is the voice of conversion, the voice of genuine evangelization. We are given great hope when priests know how to motivate others, and that's what Rafael did just two days ago: he motivated us to do the evaluation of the vicariate of Mejicanos with a passage from the Gospel of Saint Luke. In this way we renew ourselves in our various tasks, which can sometimes be mixed in with sin, no matter how holy they may seem to be. To keep them pure and clean according to the heart of God, we need to be strict not only with others but with ourselves, as Rafael was.

Finally, this death opens to us the perspectives of tran-scendence and the absolute. Now that Rafael has died, his words can no longer be confused with the voices of this earth. Perhaps slander or misunderstanding led people to confuse his voice with the voices of those seeking only earthly liberation, but now in the light of his death we can understand that his message lifts us beyond history and be-yond earthly realities. His death is not silence. His death is a most eloquent voice. It is not only the voice of his blood, which has drenched the earth, but also the voice of his spirit, which has soared to heaven and from there speaks to us: "Work to the point of leaving blood in the streets, but die with a hope that rescues your spirit for God alone." Let it be so.

---

3. CELAM, Medellín, "Peace," par. 14b.

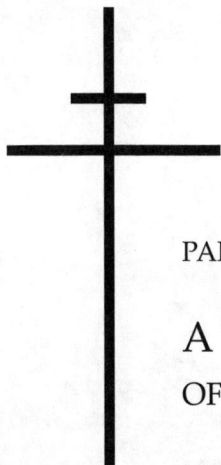

PART V

A True Church
of the Poor

The Poverty of the Beatitudes as the Force for Peoples' True Liberation

(February 17, 1980)

Romero's homilies in the second half of 1979 regularly speak of a "national crisis." The violence that took so many lives in June—including that of Father Rafael Palacios —continued to increase. In August, Romero published his fourth pastoral letter, "The Church's Mission amid the National Crisis." In this final and longest pastoral letter, Romero again put forth his vision for the archdiocese in response to the myriad challenges facing the Church: widespread suffering, an intransigent government, a repressive military, disunity among bishops, structural injustice, acts of terrorism, the specter of violent revolution, and more. He insisted that a Church must continue to proclaim the Good News of salvation and defend human dignity in the land of El Salvador. And this must be done in clear and concrete ways. Thus, in his letter, Romero takes up the task to name the sin and idols of his society, to analyze the realities of violence and Marxism, and to develop a pastoral ministry of accompaniment for Salvadorans in every sector of society. But Romero was also clear that the letter did not represent his own vision alone. He continued to live out his episcopal motto, *"Sentir con la Iglesia,"* to feel and think with the Church. He insisted that his vision was nothing more than a faithful application of Vatican II, Medellín, and more recently, the gathering of Latin American bishops in Puebla, Mexico in early 1979. Indeed, he frames the pastoral letter as the official archdiocesan reception and application of the final document of Puebla. And the pastoral letter also represented his continued listening to his people. In order to respond to the crises facing the country, Romero took the unprecedented step of surveying the priests of the dioceses as well as the lay base communities in order to guide his message.[1]

In the fall of 1979, Romero and many others saw a glimmer of hope for the political future of the country. A reform-minded group of military officers—generally referred to as the "junta"—carried out a successful coup against the government on October 15. Within a week, they installed a cabinet of prominent and respected non-military reformers and intellectuals. Romero himself was cautiously optimistic and called on the people to give the new regime time. But he also forcefully declared that the test would be if there was a decrease in violence and an investigation of past crimes.

Any hope for the new government evaporated within a couple of months. The popular organizations on the left viewed the junta with suspicion and armed revolutionary groups continued to grow. But, far more importantly, the new government could not control the military and right-wing paramilitary groups. These groups asserted their power and independence. Rather than moving toward

---

1. Many have noted how Pope Francis's emphasis on the poor and the marginalized is anticipated in the preaching and witness of Romero. In the process that Romero used for his fourth pastoral letter, we can also see something of what Francis seeks in a "synodal Church," a Church of mutual witness and encounter.

peace, the cycle of violence intensified. Repressive violence increased at a terrifying scale. By January, most of the reformers in the cabinet had resigned and the prospect of civil war became far more real.

That spring, the US Ambassador to El Salvador sent the following summary of the situation back to his superiors at the US State Department:

> The immediate threat to the junta is from the ultra-right. Backed by the great fortunes of at least some members of the oligarchy, and abetted by the acquiescence and participation of some members of the armed forces, a wave of violence against moderates has been underway for several weeks and is reaching a decisive stage. The junta must end right-wing terrorism if it is to win international support and lure away from the ultra-left those moderates who want to see structural change and an end to oppression.... For the ultra-right, it seems clear that these acts of terror are designed to eliminate or radicalize the relatively moderate elements on the left and preclude a moderate solution. For the ultra-left, the goal is to provoke rightist assassinations or a wholesale massacre that will outrage the population and kick off a national insurrection... probably the most serious threat to a moderate solution would be the assassination... of Archbishop Romero, the most important political figure in El Salvador and a symbol of a better life to the poor.[2]

---

2. Quoted in Matt Eisenbrandt, *Assassination of a Saint: The Plot to Murder Óscar Romero and the Quest to Bring His Killers to Justice* (Oakland, CA: University of California Press, 2017), 37.

Romero had made the flourishing of the poor the test of true justice and of the common good. All around he saw people committed above all else to their political ideologies, to power, or to money. In contrast, he proclaimed with force and clarity what Church teachings call "the preferential option for the poor."

The preferential option for the poor remains a foundational part of Catholic social teaching and an authentic Catholic vision for the building up of society. In official documents, it was first proclaimed by the Latin American bishops at their meeting in Puebla, Mexico in 1979 and then taken up strongly by Pope John Paul II in 1987 in his encyclical *Sollicitudo Rei Socialis*. There the pope writes, "the option or love of preference for the poor...is an option, or a special form of primacy in the exercise of Christian charity, to which the whole tradition of the Church bears witness. It affects the life of each Christian inasmuch as he or she seeks to imitate the life of Christ, but it applies equally to our social responsibilities and hence to our manner of living, and to the logical decisions to be made concerning the ownership and use of goods" (#42). Pope Benedict XVI and, quite famously, Pope Francis continued to affirm and develop these ideas in important ways.

Romero anticipated all of them. Over the three years of his preaching and ministry, the preferential option became a sort of unifying center to his thought. He came to see it as a way for the Church to remain united and faithful in the midst of tremendous division and confusion. If the Church truly proclaims the dignity of all and seeks the full flourishing of all, Romero insisted that Christians must attend preferentially (but not exclusively) to those whose dignity is trampled upon, those whose flourishing is so clearly frustrated. Such "attention" should include concrete acts of charity, but it also demands a transformation of violent and oppressive social structures. Thus, for Romero, the preferential option represented the most important foundation for Christian engagement in politics, even if the teaching is not first and foremost political.

On February 17, 1980, Romero took his cue from the gospel text for the day and offered a beautiful synthesis of his vision for the Church. The Gospels present two versions of the beatitudes of Jesus. Most familiar to most Christians is the version of Matthew which opens, "Blessed are the poor in spirit, for theirs is the kingdom of heaven" (Matt 5:3). Luke's version is sparser, sharper, and accompanied by a series of "woes." Luke's first beatitude declares, "Blessed are you who are poor, for yours is the kingdom of God...but woe to you who are rich, for you have received your consolation" (Luke 6:21, 24). Christians have traditionally read the two sets of beatitudes together, but the temptation has always been to privilege Matthew's and to read Luke's text—sometimes to the point of erasure—in light of Matthew's. But Romero always took seriously the call to proclaim God's word. And that Sunday the liturgy offered him and his people the beatitudes in Luke: "Blessed are you who are poor."

In the background of Romero's homily stand three texts—Medellín and two of Romero's own writings. You will see him quote all three extensively in his homily. We have seen Romero refer often to the texts of the Latin American Bishops' Conference at Medellín in 1968. For this homily, he uses the text on "Poverty" to structure his remarks. As always, Romero puts into practice his motto to *Sentir con la Iglesia*. From Medellín he draws a three-fold account of poverty: involuntary poverty as an evil which must be rejected; a spiritual poverty of dependence on God; and poverty as a sign of commitment to the Gospel and to the materially poor. His homily remains one of the most insightful commentaries on this central text from Medellín.

Two weeks before this homily, Romero traveled to Belgium to receive an honorary doctorate from the University of Louvain. There he gave one of his most important addresses, "The Political Dimension of Faith from the Perspective of the Option for the Poor." Romero concludes his address with an appeal to a phrase from the early Church: *Gloria Dei vivens homo*—the glory of God is the living human being. God's goodness and beauty are seen in the dignity of the human person and that person's full flourishing. But Romero notes that this vision could be made more concrete in today's world: *Gloria Dei vivens pauper*—the glory of God is the living poor person, the poor person fully alive. For Romero, this is the vision of the Gospel. This should guide all Christian involvement in society and politics. While keeping everyone's dignity and flourishing in mind, the central political question—*if we truly care about all*—should be how to construct a society that ensures life, dignity, agency, and flourishing for the poor and marginalized. In this way, he says, "The Church's option for the poor explains the political dimension of the faith in its fundamentals and in its basic outline." Here Christians find the key to living out their priestly, prophetic, and royal calling in the world.

Romero mentions—and indeed reads in full—a third text near the conclusion of the homily. In the 1970s and 1980s, as with much of Latin America, El Salvador found itself existing in a world significantly defined by the Cold War and US policy to resist any advance of communism in the western hemisphere. The Salvadoran military received significant training and financial support from the US, and this would continue through the time of the Salvadoran Civil War (1980–1992). Indeed, US-trained counter-insurgency battalions carried out some of the worst atrocities of the Civil War, from the horrific massacre of more than eight hundred villagers in El Mozote in 1981 to the execution-style killing of the eight martyrs of the University of Central America in 1989—six Jesuit priests, their housekeeper, and her daughter. In 1980, Romero found it impossible to speak the word of God into Salvadoran reality while simply ignoring the military aid that enabled so much of the violence. Thus, he took the bold step of writing directly to President Jimmy Carter, appealing to him as a Christian and as a defender of human rights around the globe. Romero called upon Carter to stop the flow of lethal aid into his small country, to stop enabling so much of the death and violence that dominated the country. Romero read that letter at Mass on February 17, receiving great applause and approval from his people.

Suggestions for Further Reading

Romero's homilies in the final months of 1979 and the opening of 1980 speak to the urgency and challenges facing the Salvadoran Church. Any of these homilies would be helpful further reading. However, two other texts already mentioned above deserve special attention.

- Fourth Pastoral Letter, "The Church's Mission amid the National Crisis" (August 6, 1979) in

Voice of the Voiceless: The Four Pastoral Letters and Other Statements, trans. Michael J. Walsh (Orbis Books, 1985), 125–176.

– Louvain Address, "The Political Dimension of the Faith from the Perspective of the Option for the Poor" (February 2, 1980) in *Voice of the Voiceless*, 193–204.

Dear sisters and brothers, before anything I want to congratulate you for impressing on this moment the true identity of the people of God. I'm referring to a comment made to me last Sunday by an elderly Venezuelan politician who spent some time with us and was rather curious. He thought our Masses resembled political meetings and that people were coming to them out of political curiosity. Though misrepresenting our Sunday Mass, this man, who is a great Christian besides being a politician, told me, "Still, I realized that it is a true Christian assembly because the people pray and sing. What impressed me tremendously was the great procession of people who approached the Eucharist at the moment of communion." I felt a very intense joy because I am in no way attempting to practice politics. If I shed some light on the politics of my country because the moment calls for it, I do so as a pastor, using the light of the Gospel. As Church we have the obligation to illuminate the paths the country is taking and to make whatever contribution we can.

I am grateful to you, then, for giving to this gathering the identity of God's people. As God's people, you live in the midst of the "natural" people of our land, and you feel responsible for meditating on the Gospel so that each of you can go forth and, according to your circumstance, be a multiplier of the word, shining light on the paths of the nation. The circumstances always lend themselves to this. Indeed, what circumstance is not appropriate if the Gospel is the incarnation of God in all human circumstances? At this time when our country is experiencing fear, confusion, insecurity, and uncertainty, we are badly in need of a calming word whose reach is infinite: the Gospel.

This Sunday we meet up with another circumstance: we are about to begin Lent. As people of God we cannot forget our liturgical journey. Today we have reached the Sixth Sunday of Ordinary Time. These past six Sundays of Ordinary Time have come between the feast of the Epiphany and the beginning of Lent. At this point Ordinary Time will be interrupted because next Wednesday we'll enter into another intense season of our liturgical year, the season that includes Lent, Easter, and Pentecost. At Pentecost we will finish celebrating the fifty days of the Easter season, and we'll return to Ordinary Time with its Seventh Sunday. But I think this present moment, as we take leave of Ordinary Time and prepare for Lent, is ideal for disposing ourselves as people of God to enter with all our hearts into the great, all-embracing spiritual retreat called Lent.

Next Wednesday, Ash Wednesday, we will inaugurate the season of Lent. Right here, God willing, we will inaugurate the season of Lent at seven o'clock on Wednesday. I invite all of you who can attend to be here for the impressive ceremony of the ashes, which are a sign of our mortality but also of our "supernaturality." Let us use this time for serious reflection. I don't think that there is any time more valuable for helping the country than the season of Lent, if we experience it as a great campaign of prayer and penance. We are not politicians, nor do we trust in purely human forces. We are first of all Christians, and we know that "if the Lord does not build our civilization, all those who build it labor in vain"

(Ps 127:1). We know, therefore, that our power comes from prayer and from conversion to God.

So let us make good use of this time to prepare for our long pilgrimage. We begin our journey on Wednesday and continue until Easter and Pentecost, the two great goals of Lent. People do not mortify themselves out of a perverse desire to suffer. God did not make us for suffering. If we fast and do penance and pray, it is because we have a very positive goal that will be reached by overcoming ourselves. Our goal is Easter, the resurrection, but we don't just celebrate a Christ who rises and is somehow different from us. During Lent we prepare ourselves to rise with him to a new life; we prepare ourselves to be the new men and women that our country so badly needs today. Let us not just cry out for a change of structures, because new structures are useless when no new persons are available to manage and enliven those structures that the country so urgently needs.[1]

After Easter we have Pentecost, the coming of the Holy Spirit. Let us prepare ourselves so that our hearts will be like spotless vessels, ready for when the Spirit of God comes with all his sanctifying power to transform the face of the earth. That is what is needed in our country: much Spirit of God, much sense of resurrection, much renewal of life.

So Lent invites us to look within and to renew ourselves, and that's just what I think today's readings are: a call to interior renewal and a wonderful prologue to Lent. I think we find in the Puebla document a statement that fills us with hope if we really understand it: "In Latin America poverty is a palpable reality marking the lives of the great mass of people, but at the same time these people are open to

---

1. CELAM, Medellín, "Justice," par. 3.

receiving the blessings and the loving devotion of the Father and are capable of being the genuine protagonists of their own development."[2] The poor are a sign in Latin America. The great majority in our countries are poor, and that is why they are able to receive these gifts from God. Because they are filled with God, they are capable of transforming their own societies. What I like about Puebla is that it also says that young people, along with the poor, are a sign. Beloved youth, you are clear signs of God's presence in Latin America, just like the poor!

"The poor and the young are the treasure and the hope of the Church in Latin America, so that evangelizing them is a priority."[3] That means that our Church feels a special affection and a special responsibility for the poor majority and for the young. Let us be confident that the poor and the young are going to rebuild our country. Let us prepare ourselves as people who are poor and youthful, as most of our people are. The resurrection of the Lord will be revealed in those two great signs, the poor and the young, the only elements capable of rebuilding El Salvador. Let us not lose hope. If they are the hope of Latin America, then in El Salvador there is tremendous hope because there are many poor and many young people.

Therefore, I'm going to take the title of my homily today from a text of the Medellín documents that speaks about poverty and says that poverty is a denunciation, a spirit, and a commitment.[4] The general title states the theme of the homily: "The Poverty of the Beatitudes as the Force for the True Liberation of the People." The three points for reflection are

---

2. CELAM, Puebla, par. 1129.

3. CELAM, Puebla, par. 1132.

4. CELAM, Medellín, "The Poverty of the Church," par. 4.

those indicated by Medellín. The Beatitudes are a force for liberation, first, because poverty is a divine denunciation; second, because poverty is a spirit; and third, because poverty is a commitment. Today, God willing, we'll have a clearer idea of what we so often repeat, namely, that the Church has made a preferential option for the poor and that she can be the true Church only if she is converted and commits herself to the poor and suffering people.

Poverty Is a Divine Denunciation

First, there is what Medellín says about poverty as a denunciation, which I'm going to back up with today's liturgical texts. Medellín states, "Insofar as it is a lack of goods of this world, poverty is an evil." So, lacking the goods of the world is an evil. "The prophets condemn it as contrary to the will of the Lord and as generally the fruit of human injustice and sin."[5]

What else was Jesus saying in the gospel account of the Beatitudes? How delightful it is to be reflecting today with that Jesus who "comes down" to a level place (Luke 6:17). The gospel expressions help us to get a deeper understanding of Jesus. Let us watch him coming down from the mountain to mix in on the plain with the common folk. Once down on the plain, he talks to the people, uttering the first words of this gospel: "Blessed are you who are poor, for the kingdom of God is yours" (Luke 6:20b).

In addition to pronouncing these four Beatitudes, Jesus explains why there are poor people, why there are people who are hungry, why there are people who suffer. They are blessed since they suffer and weep and hunger, but why do they exist? Today's gospel points out bluntly the causes of

---

5. CELAM, Medellín, "The Poverty of the Church," par. 4a.

these problems: "Woe to you who are rich, because you have received your consolation! Woe to you who are filled now, for you will be hungry! Woe to you who laugh now, for you will grieve and weep!" (Luke 6:24–25). The voice of Christ resounds with the message of all the Old Testament prophets. The prophets are fierce in their denunciations of "those who join house to house and land to land in order to become owners of the whole country" (Isa 5:8).

When poverty exists as the lack of what is necessary, sisters and brothers, it is an accusation. Some people claim that the misery in our country is being caused by the Church and the bishop, but they are trying to cover up the reality. The ones who have caused great evil are those who have created the conditions that make our people suffer such horrendous social injustice. It is therefore the poor who have marked out the true path for the Church. A Church that does not join with the poor and denounce with them the injustices visited upon them is not the true Church of Jesus Christ.

I want to use this opportunity to tell you that this was precisely the theme of my discourse at the University of Louvain. Since they told me that the general theme for this year's conferences at that famed university was "politics and faith," I chose to develop the theme by speaking on "the political dimension of faith from the perspective of the poor." I tried to explain to them how, for us here in El Salvador, the key for understanding Christian faith is the poor. I told them there in Louvain, "Our Salvadoran world is not an abstraction. It is not just another case of what you in the developed countries understand by "world." Our world is one in which the great majority of men and women are poor and oppressed. Moreover, we are saying that that world of the poor is the key for understanding Christian faith, Church action, and the political dimension of that faith and that Church action. The poor are the ones who tell us what the world really is and what kind of service the Church should be rendering to the world. The poor are the ones who tell us what politics is. The origin of the word "politics" is *polis*, which means "city," and the poor tell us what the *polis* is, what the city is, and what it means for the Church to live in the world, in the *polis*, in the city. "Allow me," I told them, "to briefly explain from the perspective of the poor of my people, whom I seek to represent, the situation and the action of our Church in the world in which we live." So I began to tell them about the adventure of our Church in El Salvador and about what it is we are doing.

First of all, we immerse ourselves among the poor. We want a Church that truly is close to the poor people of El Salvador, and what we notice as we draw close to the poor is that we discover in them the true face of the Suffering Servant of Yahweh. That is where we come to know most intimately the mystery of the Christ who takes on flesh and becomes poor for our sake.

What else does the Church do here? I told them that we announce the Good News to the poor, but not demagogically so as to exclude other people. To the contrary, I told them, "The people who for ages have heard only bad news and who have experienced even worse realities are now, through the Church, hearing the announcement of Jesus: "The kingdom of God is near at hand; it is yours" (Mark 1:15). "Blessed are you poor, for the kingdom of God is yours" (Luke 6:20b). And since that is true, there is also Good News for the wealthy: that they, by being converted to the poor, can share with them the treasures of God's kingdom, which belongs to the poor."

Another thing about the Church in El Salvador, I told them, is her commitment to defending the poor. "The poor majority of our country finds in the Church the voice of the prophets of Israel. Among us there are those who 'sell the just for money and the poor for a pair of sandals,' as the prophet said (Amos 8:6). There are 'those who store up violence and booty in their palaces' (Amos 3:10); there are 'those who crush the poor' (Amos 8:4); there are 'those who bring on a reign of violence while reclining on beds of ivory' (Amos 6:3b–4); there are 'those who join house to house and field to field so as to take up all there is and remain alone in the land' (Isa 5:8). These words of the prophets are not distant voices that we read with reverence in our liturgy. They are ever-present realities whose cruelty and vehemence we experience day by day."

For this reason, I told them, the Church suffers the fate of the poor, which is persecution. Our Church is happy that the blood of her priests, her catechists, and her communities has been mingled with the blood of our massacred people and that she has always carried the mark of persecution. It is precisely because of her protests that people malign her and refuse to hear her voice calling out against injustice. This is the political dimension of faith.

The second part of my discourse dealt with the ways in which the Church has been enriched in her political understanding of the people and the poor, which has helped the Church to gain a clearer sense of the meaning of sin. And that is precisely what we are saying here today, that poverty is a condemnation of sin. By drawing close to the poor, the Church understands the true gravity of sin: "Sin is what killed the Son of God, and sin is what continues to kill God's children. We see that basic truth of the faith daily in the situation of our country. We cannot offend God without offending our brothers and sisters. Therefore it is not out of routine that we once again affirm the existence of structures of sin in our country. The structures are sinful because they produce the fruits of sin, the death of Salvadorans, whether it's a swift death or the slow death of structural oppression. That is why we have denounced the sin of injustice."

This mystery of poverty also helps us to understand better the redemption of Jesus Christ who became like us in all things in order to redeem us from our sins. The mystery of poverty also helps us to understand God better. God wants to give us life, and anyone who destroys or damages life— by mutilating, by torturing, by repressing—is revealing to us also in some way the contrasting divine image of the God of life, the God who respects human freedom.

This is the first reflection for today's homily, and I'm happy to have been able to express these ideas in a highly organized country like Belgium. I wanted to help them understand what is very difficult to understand in that setting: a Church that does not get involved in politics but that, by drawing on the prophetic word of God, denounces injustice in the reality experienced by the poor, a reality which speaks for itself.

Poverty is holy also because it cries out and denounces our own Church. Puebla itself expresses this thought: "Commitment to the poor and oppressed and the rise of the base communities have helped the Church to discover the evangelizing potential of the poor. The poor challenge the Church constantly, calling her to conversion and demonstrating in their own lives, as many of them do, the evangelical values of solidarity, service, simplicity, and readiness to accept the gift of God."[6] Everyone who denounces must be ready to be denounced. If the Church denounces injustice, she is also ready to hear herself accused and is obliged to seek conversion. The

---

6. Puebla, par. 1147.

poor are constantly crying out, denouncing not only social injustice but also the scant generosity of our own Church.

Poverty Is a Spirit

So poverty is first of all a denunciation, but the second thing
I want to say today is that poverty is a spirit. What Medellín
says in this regard I find very interesting: "Spiritual poverty
is the theme of the poor of Yahweh. Spiritual poverty is the
attitude of openness to God, the ready disposition of those
who hope for everything from the Lord. Although we may
value the goods of this world, we remain free of them and
recognize the higher values of the goods of the kingdom."[7]

Poverty is therefore a spirituality and an attitude that
opens up a Christian's soul to God. That is why Puebla said
that the poor are the hope of Latin America; it is because they
are more disposed to receive God's gifts. And that is why
Christ said with such emotion, "Blessed are you who are
poor, for the kingdom of God is yours" (Luke 6:20b). You are
the ones most able to understand what is not understood by
those who are on their knees before false idols, placing their
trust in them. You do not have those idols nor do you trust in
them because you have no wealth and no power. You are
completely dispossessed, but the poorer you are, the more
you possess the kingdom of God as long as you truly embrace this spirituality. The poverty sanctified here by Jesus
Christ is not simply material poverty, for not having anything
is an evil. He is talking about poverty that is fully aware,
poverty that accepts the cross and sacrifice, not out of resig-
nation but with the knowledge that such is God's will. To the
degree that we make our poverty a source of awareness,

---

7. Medellín, "Poverty of the Church," par. 4b.

spirituality, and generous commitment to the Lord, we become holy, and holiness will make us better liberators of our people. The Church is shaping these liberators of the people. To the extent that you as Christians convert your poverty into spirituality, you become liberators of our people.

Consider the moment when Christ spoke that Beatitude so that we can see its meaning. We shouldn't remove it from its context in the long history of Israel. How was Israel born? It was born from God's promise to an old man called Abraham. Both he and his wife were barren and without children, but God told him, "From your descendants I am going to make a great people" (Gen 12:2). Israel began under a sign of poverty and complete limitation: they could not have children, but God told them that he would give them a whole people as descendants. Abraham accepted God's word by faith, and that people truly became a reality. That people in turn were then promised by God, "I am going to give you a land" (Gen 12:7). Then, under the leadership of Moses, God led them to the Promised Land. In the Promised Land God offered the people his law and his covenant, but they were not faithful. Because of their infidelity the people went into exile, where they lamented the blessings that God had given them but that had been taken away because of their sin. This was still another sign of poverty. "Now you must repent", God told them. The prophets called the people to repentance, and they obtained God's pardon. Returning from Babylon, the people rejoiced to be in their own country again, but there were still many political vicissitudes. What is of interest to us now is that at one point the Roman Empire took possession of that land and dominated it by their administration and their army. They were a dominated people! It was to that people dominated by Rome that Christ came. It was to that people politically subject to the imperialism of a foreign power that Christ preached this Beatitude we heard today: "Blessed are you who are poor, for the kingdom of God is yours" (Luke 6:20b).

I have recalled this context to keep us from spiritualizing the Beatitudes of the Gospel, because Saint Matthew offers us a reflection that is more difficult to understand: "Blessed are the poor in spirit," he tells us (Matt 5:3). Many people have twisted this phrase so as to make it mean that everybody is poor, even those who are oppressing others. That is not true. In the context of Matthew's Gospel, the "poor in spirit"—or simply the "poor," as Luke has it—are those who experience scarcity, those who are suffering oppression; they are people who need God to escape from their plight.

Jesus Christ does not arrive with weapons or revolutionary political movements, but he does teach us that all earthly revolutions can play a part in freeing us from sin and leading us to eternal life. He provides a wider horizon for those who are struggling for the liberation of the people. When Christ spoke about the "poor in spirit," he was referring to the Israelites, and he understood their love of their homeland. He was telling them, "You must be free again. You must one day shake off the yoke of those who have invaded this land, but you must adopt this spirituality of the poor in order to do so."

The Virgin Mary, the person most filled with the Spirit of Yahweh, understood this when she sang in her Magnificat about how God frees the lowly and the poor. An explicit political dimension is sounded when Mary declares that "God sent the rich away empty and filled the poor with good things" (Luke 1:53). She even uttered words that today would be called "insurrectional": "He dethrones rulers when they work against the peace of the people" (Luke 1:52). This is the political dimension of our faith as experienced by Mary and by Jesus. Jesus was a true patriot in a nation that was under foreign domination, a nation that he doubtlessly wanted to see freed. Until then, though, there was a need to pay tribute to Caesar: "Grant to Caesar what belongs to Caesar, but do not give to Caesar what belongs to God. Give to God what belongs to God!" (Mark 12:17).

This is the spirituality that the first reading this Sunday has proposed quite explicitly. When Christ spoke, he no doubt was recalling the sayings of the ancient prophets, just as the Church today reads an Old Testament passage together with a text of the Gospel of Christ. We also hear—along with the Beatitudes of the poor, the hungry, the suffering, the mourning—an echo of Jeremiah: "Cursed are those who trust in human beings and who seek strength in flesh while turning their hearts from the Lord. Like barren bushes in the desert, they will not prosper; they grow in a parched desert, on salty and inhospitable earth" (Jer 17:5–6). Such is the arid state of those who place their confidence in the things of earth. That is why you rich are to be pitied. Even if now you appear to be thriving trees, tomorrow you will be dry stumps in the arid desert because of your selfish ways. The message of the prophets is a great contrast: "Blessed are those who trust in the Lord!" Doesn't this seem to you to echo Christ's words, "Blessed are the poor who trust in the Lord?" The prophet says, "Blessed are those who place their trust in the Lord, for they are like trees that are planted near water and stretch out their roots to the stream. When hot weather comes, they do not feel it; their leaves stay green. In the year of drought they show no distress but still bear fruit" (Jer 17:7–8).

These are the people who are truly poor. The spirituality of those who are poor is centered on having great trust in the Lord. Woe descends upon the rich when they draw apart from the Lord and place their trust in the flesh, that is, in earthly values. So the prestige of the Church, sisters and brothers, does not come from pleasing the powerful. The prestige of the

Church comes when the poor feel that the Church is theirs; it comes from giving the Church an earthly dimension that calls out to everyone, the rich included, to be converted and saved through the poor, for only the poor are uniquely blessed.

Regarding this question of poverty of spirit, I want to reflect on today's second reading because it gives us a basis for our hope. It is from Paul's letter to the Christians of Corinth, where there were some erroneous ideas about the resurrection. People were saying that there was no resurrection, and they made fun of Paul when he spoke about the resurrection. So Paul tried to strengthen their faith. Remember what Paul told us last Sunday: "There are witnesses to the risen Christ, including five hundred disciples. And last of all he appeared also to me, the one who is speaking to you. I was persecuting the Church and was not at all disposed to believe what they were saying about the Church, but I have seen him, I was converted, and now I am preaching him" (1 Cor 15:6–9).

Saint Paul is a marvelous witness of the resurrection because, if there was ever a person who did not want to believe in Jesus or in the resurrection, it was the persecutor Saul. He thought the Christians were deceiving their fellow Jews, and that's why he persecuted them. Even though Paul was convinced that Christ was not alive, once the living Christ appeared to him, he was ready to give his life for this great truth. He told the Corinthians with the erroneous ideas, "You are wrong. Christ has risen! And if you say that the dead do not rise, why have I seen the risen Christ? Why does the risen Christ exist? But if Christ has risen, then there is resurrection for all. If there is resurrection, then our faith and our hope are well grounded. For if Christ had not risen, then we would be the most miserable of people, believing in a lie!" (1 Cor 15:20). But Christ has risen! Christ lives, and this is the great belief and trust, the great spirituality of the poor. This is our God, the God of the poor, as our popular hymn puts it.[8]

Poverty Is a Commitment

As my final reflection for today, I want to leave you with this idea: poverty is a force for liberation because, besides being a denunciation of sin and a key element of Christian spirituality, it is also a commitment.

Fellow Christians, this truth first of all applies to me, who must give an example of being Christian, but it also applies to you, dear fellow priests, religious, and all of you who are baptized and call yourselves Christian. Here is what Medellín says: "Poverty is a commitment by which one voluntarily and lovingly takes on the condition of the needy of this world in order to bear witness to the evil which poverty represents and to declare one's spiritual freedom with regard to material goods. Such poverty follows the example of Christ who assumed all the consequences of our sinful condition and who "being rich became poor" (2 Cor 8:9) in order to redeem us."[9] This is our commitment as Christians: following Christ in his incarnation. If Christ as the God of majesty became a lowly human and lived with the poor and suffered the death of slaves on the cross, so also should be our own Christian faith. Any Christian who does not want to make that commitment of solidarity with the poor is not worthy to be called Christian.

This tremendous doctrine is confirmed in today's gospel, when Christ tells us not to fear persecution. Because—believe

---

8. *"Vos sos el Dios de los pobres"* ["Your are the God of the poor"], entrance hymn of the *Misa Campesina Nicaraguense* of Carlos Mejía Godoy, 1975.

9. Medellín, "Poverty of the Church," 4c.

me, sisters and brothers—those who commit themselves to the poor must experience the same fate as the poor. And in El Salvador we know what the fate of the poor is: being disappeared, being tortured, being arrested, being found dead.

If you want the privileges of this world instead of the persecutions that come with commitment to the poor, then listen to the awesome antithesis of today's gospel: "Blessed are you when people hate you and when they exclude and insult you and denounce your name as evil on account of the Son of Man. Rejoice and leap for joy on that day because your reward will be great in heaven!" (Luke 6:22–23). With great joy and gratitude I want to commend our priests. The more committed they are with the poor, the more maligned they are; the more committed they are with the misery of our people, the more reviled they are. I want to rejoice also with the religious women and men who are committed to this people and who suffer with them heroically. I rejoice with the Christian communities and the catechists who stay in their posts while others flee in fear.

Those who wish to flee because of persecution, calumny, and humiliation should hear what Christ declares this Sunday: "Woe to you when all speak well of you for that was how your ancestors treated the false prophets" (Luke 6:26). How sad is the adulation of the world! If Christians who are suffering slander and persecution want to be treated well, then they would do better to betray their Christian faith and live on their knees before money, for that is how the well-regarded of this world live. But woe to you!

Today's second reading also confirms this truth about poverty as commitment. The most extreme manifestations of poverty are sin and death. No people are more miserable than those who are in sin, and no being is poorer than a corpse, but it was to these that Christ committed himself, the sinners and the dead. That is why Christ's redemption marks all forms of earthly liberation as deficient; they are not complete since they cannot free sinners from sin or the dead from death. This is what the great Liberator offers us. Blessed therefore are those who work for political liberation on earth while keeping in mind the redemption brought by Christ, who saves us from sin and from death.

Today's second reading strengthens the hearts of a people struggling to rise from the dead. Believe in the resurrection! Do not doubt that Christ has risen and that by his cross and his glory he has saved us from the sin and the death that afflict humankind. We will all die, but those who believe in Christ will not be dead forever. There in heaven we will sing of the triumph of immortality, and all the struggles for earthly liberation will seem to us like minor skirmishes. The greatest liberation is Christ's, and all those who join the freedom struggle of their people to faith in Christ will be guaranteed integral, complete, and immortal liberation. Do not be like those who draw apart from this Christian liberation and struggle only for temporal things, such as better wages, cheaper goods, different politicians, and new structures that tomorrow will be old. All those things are temporal and transitory, but when one works for them with a Christian spirit, then that stays in the soul.

So all of you who are in organized groups or political parties, don't forget this: if you are Christians, live intensely this spirituality of poverty, and live intensely this Christian commitment to the poor! There are many of you in the struggle, thank God, and many of you arose from our ecclesial communities. What is regrettable is that many have lost their faith and have failed in what is most important. But there are those of you who continue to struggle in the people's political organizations without betraying your faith. You still look to your Christian communities to nourish your struggle with faith and to test your political judgments by faith. In this you do well.

That is what I wanted to say in my fourth pastoral letter when I stated that one of the most urgent needs of the pastoral ministry of the archdiocese today is the ministry of accompaniment.[10] That means helping to bring to maturity the faith of the women and men in political groups, so that they remain fully committed without betraying the faith. They should know that the faith has a political dimension, but it is still always faith in the eternal resurrection of the Lord and our being saved from sin. Let us hope that the Church will not be demeaned when she draws on faith to cry out against the deficiencies, the abuses, the strategies, or the limitations of the political groups. Do not reject her. Listen to her as a mother; listen to her as a teacher of the faith if you truly want to do honor to your Christian identity. Be true to the title "Christian" because it is no use being called a Christian if you are not really Christian.

Life of the Church

Our desire is to create a Church like the one Christ has described for us today, a Church of the poor but not defined by social class. She is a Church of the poor because she saves all who want to be saved by our embrace of the poor. Let us try to make our archdiocese this kind of Church, sisters and

---

10. "The Church's Mission in the Midst of the Nation's Crisis" (August 6, 1979), sections 92–94.

brothers. The information I'm going to give you now is precisely for that purpose.

I already made the announcement about Lent at the start, but now I repeat my invitation for us all to come together here next Wednesday at seven in the evening to inaugurate Lent in a solemn manner. Since many people in the villages will be hearing this announcement by radio, I want to repeat for them what Father Fabián Amaya already announced on Friday, namely, that in the communities where there is no priest, someone will be authorized to go to receive the blessed ashes at the parish Mass and bring them back to the communities. Then the person in charge of the community—whether a lay man or woman or a sister—will celebrate the Ash Wednesday service, which consists mainly in an invitation to conversion. In the archdiocesan offices we'll have copies of the text of the service, and anyone who wishes can get a free copy. Everything that needs to be done is written there.

If you can't get a copy of the text, then just read some passage from the Bible and explain the meaning of Lent and the meaning of the imposition of ashes. Let us welcome this Lent humbly as we hear Christ tell us that the kingdom of God is near and we should be converted to the Gospel (Mark 1:15). But nobody should be left out. If you're unable even to join your village community, then do the ceremony in your homes. The father of the family can take a bit of ashes and celebrate the beginning of Lent with his family; he can impose the holy ashes since he is the true priest of the family. It's not a sacrament but simply a rite that reminds us: "You are dust, and unto dust you shall return." The important thing is being converted to the Lord. We want this beautiful rite to reach every home, and we sincerely ask everyone to collaborate in celebrating the start of Lent and to do so as widely as possible. Let us all truly enter into a season of conversion, prayer, fasting, and penance.

> [Romero continued this section with a discussion of fasting during Lent, preparing for Easter, and other events in the life of the Church.]

Events of the Week

Now, from the vantage point of the Church, which must be light for the world, we look toward the world that surrounds us so as to illuminate it with faith. When I spoke in Louvain about the political dimension of the faith, I concluded by saying that the limits of the political dimension of faith are marked out for our Church precisely by the world of the poor. In all the different political junctures, what most concerns us is the people who are poor. I told them, "I don't want to go into all the various details of my country's politics. I prefer to explain to you the profound roots of the Church's activity in the explosive sociopolitical world of El Salvador. And I want to make clear to you that the ultimate theological and historical criterion for the Church's activity in this area is the world of the poor." What I told them, then, is that the Church is doing just as we say in this homily: it is supporting all that benefits the poor as well as denouncing all that is bad for the poor.

Using this norm, we are going to judge some things that happened this week. For example, they promulgated the famous decree 114, which has aroused much discussion and polemic. The Church is not interested in legalities, which are often a cover for self-interest. What interests the Church is whether that decree is really going to move us toward the transformations that the poor need or whether it will fail to lead in that direction. If the decree means something good for the poor, the Church is in agreement. If it means nothing for the poor, then it is of no interest to the Church.

. . .

The present government has no popular support and depends only on the armed forces and certain foreign powers. This is another serious failure on the part of the Christian Democrats: their presence in the government, along with particular political and economic interests, is inducing countries like Venezuela and the United States to support an alternative that they claim is anti-oligarchy but is in fact anti-people. This concern has moved me to be bold enough to write a letter to President Carter himself, and I am going to send it to him after you give me your opinion of it.

Mr. President:

In the last few days, news has appeared in the national press that worries me greatly. According to the reports, your government is studying the possibility of economic and military support and assistance to the present government junta.

Because you are a Christian and because you have shown that you want to defend human rights, I venture to set forth for you my pastoral point of view in regard to this news and to make a specific request of you.

I am very concerned by the news that the government of the United States is planning to exacerbate

El Salvador's arms race by sending military equipment and advisors to "train three Salvadoran battalions in logistics, communications, and intelligence." If this information from the papers is correct, your government's contribution, instead of favoring greater justice and peace in El Salvador, will undoubtedly aggravate the injustice and the repression against the organized forces of the people who have been struggling to have their most basic human rights respected.

The present government junta and its backers in the armed forces and other security forces have unfortunately not demonstrated a capacity to resolve in practice the nation's serious political and structural problems. For the most part, they have resorted to repressive violence, producing a total of deaths and injuries much greater than under the previous military regime, whose systematic violation of human rights was reported by the InterAmerican Commission on Human Rights.

The brutal form in which the security forces recently evicted and murdered the persons occupying the offices of the Christian Democratic Party, even though the operation was not authorized by the junta or the party, is an indication that the junta and the Christian Democrats do not govern the country. Rather, political power is in the hands of unscrupulous military officers who are interested only in repressing the people and favoring the interests of the Salvadoran oligarchy.

If it is true that last November a "group of six Americans was in El Salvador, providing $200,000 in gas masks and flak jackets and teaching agents how to use them against demonstrators," you should be informed that since that time the security forces, counting on increased personal protection and efficiency, have been even more violent in repressing the people with deadly weapons.

For this reason, given that as a Salvadoran and as archbishop of the Archdiocese of San Salvador I have an obligation to see that faith and justice reign in my country, I ask you, if you truly want to defend human rights:
- to forbid that military aid be given to the Salvadoran government, and
- to guarantee that your government will not intervene directly or indirectly, by means of military, economic, diplomatic, or other pressures, in determining the destiny of the Salvadoran people.

In these moments, we are living through a grave economic and political crisis in our country, but it is certain that the people are becoming more aware and more organized and that they have begun to prepare themselves to manage and take responsibility for the future of El Salvador, for they are the only ones capable of overcoming the crisis. It would be unjust and deplorable for foreign powers to intervene and frustrate the Salvadoran people, to repress them and keep them from freely deciding the economic and political course that our nation should follow.

It would constitute the violation of a right that the Latin American bishops, meeting at Puebla, recognized publicly when we spoke of "the legitimate self-determination of our peoples, by which they organize their society according to their own spirit and the course of their history and so cooperate in a new international order."[11]

I hope that your religious sentiments and your feelings for the defense of human rights will move you to accept my petition, thus avoiding greater bloodshed in this suffering country.

What I ask of the Christian Democrats is not only that they analyze their doubtless very good intentions but that they also examine the real effect their presence in government is having. Their support is covering up the present government's repressive character, especially at the international level. As a political force of our people, they urgently need to consider how that force can best be used to help our poor: whether as an isolated, impotent part of a government controlled by repressive military officials, or as one more force included within a broad project of popular government that is sustained not by the present, hopelessly corrupt armed forces but by the majority consensus of the people.

I am not against the institution of the Armed Forces. I continue to believe that there are honest elements who give us hope for the future. I also believe that there is a need for real security forces that provide security for our people. However, I cannot agree with the military men who, by abusing their power, bring disrepute on these essential institutions and make them into instruments of repression and injustice.

. . .

---

11. Puebla, par. 505.

The most serious threat of all is that of the extreme right, which is planning a right-wing military coup. There is much talk about this, as there is about an extended general strike by private businesses. Any such action would be an unforgivable assault on our people's aspirations for justice. The ones who are sustaining the unjust order in which we live have absolutely no right to rise up in revolt. If such a scheme were to win out over the people, who are now fully conscious of what is happening, the price would be much bloodshed, and it would not succeed in drowning out the people's cry for justice. The most logical thing for the powerful oligarchs to do is to reflect with human or, if possible, Christian serenity on Christ's summons to them in the Gospel: "Woe unto you, for tomorrow you will weep!" (Luke 6:25b). To repeat the image you already know, it is better to take off your rings in advance, lest they cut off your hands! Use reason to form your human and Christian convictions. Give the people a chance to organize in a spirit of justice, and don't try to defend what is indefensible.

Finally, I have a word for the popular organizations. Yesterday YSAX commented on them eloquently when it stated, "The Revolutionary Coordinator of the Masses, as an organization promoting popular unity, is carrying out a consolidating effort, and it is trying to enter into conversation with the democratic forces because it knows that without them their national project is not viable and that gaining power would otherwise be a very costly, if not impossible, endeavor. Nevertheless, the rational political policies of their leadership are being undermined by the irrational combative actions of their followers." So I want to tell you: we defend the right of organization, and we praise your efforts at unity and openness, but we repudiate the tactics of certain groups which are being poorly led or else are ignoring their leadership.

You cannot gain credibility among people who believe in reason and justice by resorting to actions that are irrational or needlessly violent. Agitation for agitation's sake leads nowhere. The process of unity cannot be advanced through concessions extorted by force.

. . .

I make an appeal also to the people's military organizations to return to the paths of decency, reason, and human dignity. I am referring to the kidnappings, the threats, and the vendettas. People cannot take justice into their own hands. Recourse must be had to the courts. I have transmitted many pleas for endangered lives to those who can do something to help. The sins and crimes of times past do not matter when human dignity is at stake. The pope has said that violence cannot be inflicted even on those judged guilty because it ends up really being vengeance.

. . .

Let us conclude, then, as we began, by saying that there is great hope among the poor and among those who are suffering. That is why the Church, in the name of Jesus Christ, wants to remove whatever may be base among our people. My earnest denunciations, please understand, have no other purpose than to say, "We want a holy people. We want a government that truly understands the poor. We want politics that truly works for the welfare of our people and our poor." When we have that, we'll be able to say with Jesus Christ, "Blessed are the poor, for theirs is the kingdom of heaven!" (Luke 6:20b).

Lent Is the Triumph
of God's Saving Plan in History

(February 24, 1978)

February 24, 1980 was the First Sunday of Lent. That Sunday, Romero invited his people to enter fully into this season of preparation, to recommit to their identity as baptized Christians and turn back to God in penitence. Romero did not know, of course, that this Lent was a different sort of preparation for himself. As his people prepared to enter into the mystery of redemption at Easter, his own path was converging with those of the martyrs and of his crucified messiah. Exactly one month later, he would be shot at the altar.

The gospel reading for the first Sunday in Lent is always the story of the temptations of Jesus. Here Romero found the theme for his homily, a theme that reverberates in his preaching throughout the next month: the project of God versus the idolatries, sin, and violent ambitions dominating the world around him. What does it look like to carry out the project of God? Here we see so many of the fundamental themes of Romero's preaching come together into a profound message.

Christians confess their faith in the one God every Sunday when they gather. They take up and reaffirm, as Jesus did, the core belief of the Israelites in the Old Testament: "Hear, O Israel: The Lord is our God, the Lord alone!" (Deut 6:4). But who is this God that we confess? As Romero insists in seemingly every homily, the God in whom we believe is not a distant, indifferent God—"not a disincarnate God"—but rather the Lord of history who comes and calls a people. Similarly, when a Christian hears the word of God, this is precisely so that the word "may be incarnated in one's life." The word of God is given so that one can conform one's life to it and contribute to the project of God.

And this project should be distinguished from those of the world in at least two ways. First, we have a tendency to forget the lesson of the widow's mite in Luke 21:1–4: "[Jesus] looked up and saw rich people putting their gifts into the treasury; he also saw a poor widow put in two small copper coins. He said, 'Truly I tell you, this poor widow has put in more than all of them, for all of them have contributed out of their abundance, but she out of her poverty has put in all she had to live on.'" The project of God is carried forth as much by small acts of love and devotion, perhaps hidden from the world, as it is by the grand acts that make the news. The Christian life isn't ostentatious. As Romero will tell his people, faithfulness to the project of God is to be "found in the simplicity of those who live their ordinary lives with faith...[in] giving our simple, ordinary lives a spirit of freedom and love." The work of transformative social change obviously remains important, but the root for Romero remains the ordinary Christian incarnating God's love in the world around them.

Second, the project of God is not the only project in the world. It is not the only project demanding our allegiance.

We stand like Jesus in the desert tempted by Satan. We live in a world marked by false idols. Romero is unrelenting on this point. All around us—and perhaps within us—is a world devoted to money and power. And this is no small thing; it is not just a private, personal affair: "What terrible sacrifices are being offered to the god of power, the god of money! There are so many victims, so much blood." The Christian must "unmask" these idolatries, revealing them for what they are. As Jesus responded to Satan in the desert, those who are on their knees in adoration before power and money must be reminded of the great commandment, "You shall worship the Lord, your God."

Romero issued this call to conversion to the whole people of God: "The spoken word is useless if it just vibrates and sounds without incarnating itself in the lives of Christians. Christ's greatest concern is that we Christians be truly a living word, a light for the world, and salt of the earth." But we find in his Lenten homilies of 1980 a more direct turn to the oligarchy. This was not entirely new. In 1978, in his third pastoral letter, he already made clear his view that the oligarchy represented the "main obstacle" to moving forward to a more just society.[1] Yet, in the face of the failed reforms of the new government, increasing repression from the military, and the impunity of right-wing paramilitary groups aligned with the oligarchy, Romero insists on the need for their profound conversion that Lent:

> Since we are now in the season of Lent, which is a time for conversion and reflection on what it means to be Christian, I want to make a fraternal, pastoral

---

1. Óscar Romero, *Voice of the Voiceless: The Four Pastoral Letters and Other Statements*, trans. Michael J. Walsh (Orbis Books, 1985), 170.

appeal to the oligarchy. I ask you to be converted to
life and to use your economic power for the people's benefit instead of for the misery and ruin of
our population. If you don't want to listen to me,
then at least listen to the voice of Pope John Paul II.
This very week, at the beginning of Lent, he exhorted the Catholics of the world to give up superfluous wealth in order to help the needy and to do
this as a sign of Lenten penance.

Romero challenged the oligarchy: Why do you cling so
vigorously to your vast plantations, gathering up the gifts
of God's creation to yourself rather than allowing others to
have their share? Why do you respond with violence to any
attempt of the poor and dispossessed to seek a better life?
What makes you so fearful? Romero doesn't hold back here:
the oligarchy fears losing its power and wealth, the very
gifts Satan had promised to Jesus. And with so many people urging change, the oligarchy turns to the only god it
knows: money, which it uses to buy weapons, mercenaries,
and the government itself as a way of maintaining power.

Surveying the Salvadoran landscape, Romero certainly
had far more sympathy with the aims and hopes of the
movements of reform and even revolution. He saw the demand for social justice, for a society that respected human
dignity, as an essential part of the project of God. Romero
also recognized, following Paul VI, that insurrection can at
times be morally justified. However, Romero urges those
seeking reform never to put their trust in violence. The desire for vengeance will eat the person up from the inside
and the violence it spreads will be uncontrollable. Thus,
Romero calls for a "maturation" among the "popular

forces," a sort of self-examination that recognizes that the people do not deserve a world marked by mutual recriminations, repression, and terrorism. As we have seen of course, Romero was clear that the root of the problem was structural injustice and the intransigence of the oligarchy. The popular forces certainly had greater moral justification on their side. Yet one easily becomes consumed by vengeance; one's organization and its victory can easily become one's god.

Therefore, Romero insisted on the season of Lent as precisely what was most needed for the country. All sides, every person, needed this time of preparation and penitence, a time to reconsider their own life and the path of the country. Romero encourages his people to embrace "our Salvadoran Lent," to use this time to become more faithful servants of the project of God, servants of a true, just, and lasting peace.

Further Reading

Each of Romero's homilies from Lent of 1980 are worthy of close, careful reading. Each offers a powerful call to live out the Gospel in our contemporary world. This chapter provides his homily from the First Sunday of Lent that year. In the next chapter, you will encounter his homily from the Fifth Sunday of Lent—his final Sunday homily. His preaching from the Second, Third, and Fourth Sundays of Lent that year are highly recommended as well.

 – "Lent as God's Plan for Transfiguring the People through Christ" (March 2, 1980) in *A Prophetic*

Bishop Speaks to His People: The Complete Homilies of Archbishop Óscar Arnulfo Romero, 6 vols., trans. Joseph Owens, SJ (Convivium Press, 2015–2016), 6.318–40.

– "Conversion Is Necessary for True Liberation according to God's Plan" (March 9, 1980) in *A Prophetic Bishop Speaks*, 6.341–63.

– "The Reconciliation of All in Christ in God's Project for the True Liberation of Peoples" (March 16, 1980) in *A Prophetic Bishop Speaks*, 6.364–92.

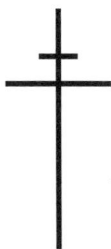

Sunday, February 24, 1980
Mass Readings
Deuteronomy 26:4–10; Romans 10:8–13
Luke 4:1–13

Dear sisters and brothers, the holy liturgy of Lent has begun, and it has an intense message for all of us who call ourselves Christian. The Second Vatican Council summed up the substance of Lent with these words: "The two elements that are especially characteristic of Lent—the recalling of baptism and the preparation for it, and penance—should be given greater emphasis in the liturgy and in liturgical catechesis. It is by means of them that the Church prepares the faithful for the celebration of Easter, while they hear God's word more frequently and devote more time to prayer."[1]

We see here, then, that Lent is preparation for the celebration of the Easter event, the death and resurrection of Christ. Easter is the feast of our redemption, and to celebrate it worthily we have a long period of spiritual preparation, which is Lent. What means are used for this preparation? The Council tells us that it is by means of baptism and penance, the two great Lenten sacraments.

Those who have not received baptism prepare to receive it on Holy Saturday evening, and those of us who have the good fortune of being already baptized must take advantage of Lent to renew the serious commitments we have as baptized Christians. If we do this, then when we celebrate

---

1. Second Vatican Council, *Sacrosanctum Concilium*, 109.

Christ's resurrection we will truly experience his death and his resurrection as our own death and our resurrection, thanks to baptism.

The second sacrament that is very important is penance, which means repenting for our sins through the official form of a sacrament in which we are told in God's name, "I absolve you from your sins."

The Council urges us to engage in intense prayer and reflection on the word of God since these are the best instruments for this grand period of preparation. Lent is therefore a time of much prayer, much Bible, much word of God. And today, which is the day when we most need to have our beloved YSAX, the instrument that carries the word of God forth from our Sunday Mass, we are sorry not to have it.

You all know that this station's transmitter was destroyed on Monday by a bomb planted by an ultra-right group.[2] This new attack is a serious violation of our freedom of expression. With this attack they are hoping to silence the prophetic and pastoral voice of the archdiocese precisely because it is trying to be the voice of those who have no voice. They want to silence it because it has been denouncing the systematic violation of human rights; it has been trying to speak the truth, to defend justice, and to spread the Christian message. Since the time of Jesus this message has scandalized the powerful; it did so then, and it does so now. And as happened then, so also now, the message is heard and accepted only by the poor and the humble folk.

I wish to use this First Sunday of Lent, when the Church earnestly bids us to hear the word of God, to protest strongly against this new act of repression which not only harms the

---

2. "Communiqué of the Office of Social Communication of the Archdiocese of San Salvador," in *Orientación* (February 24, 1980).

Church but directly affects the people. Those responsible for this attack want to prevent the people from knowing the truth and from having criteria for judging what is happening in the country. They fear the people will unite and forcefully cry out, "We have had enough! Let us put an end to the exploitation and domination of the Salvadoran oligarchy!"

Contrary to the wishes of those who want to silence our radio station, its absence on the air only serves to give greater moral vigor to the word of the Church. The solidarity that this has roused in favor of our station is something marvelous, and I want to express my sincerest thanks for it.

I never imagined that on this Sunday of Lent I would find myself being supported by a distinguished group of Brazilian bishops who sent me the following telegram.

> Archbishop Romero: We just read with great sorrow about the criminal destruction of the archdiocesan radio station. We see it as one more sign of persecution of your person, the priests, the religious, and the poor oppressed people of El Salvador. We stand in solidarity with your courageous and prophetic homily of February 17. We are grateful that you and your Church are faithfully making the preferential option for the poor. [Signed] Your brothers in the episcopate: Helder Cámara, Archbishop of Recife, Brazil; José María Pires, Archbishop of Joâo de Soa, Brazil; Samuel Ruiz, Bishop of Chiapas, Mexico; Jesús Calderón, Bishop of Puno, Peru; Pedro Casaldáliga, Bishop of San Félix, Brazil; José A. Llaguno, Apostolic Vicar of Tarahumara, Mexico; Jorge Hourton, Bishop in Chile; Tomás Balduino, Bishop of Goyas, Brazil; Marcelo Caballería, Bishop of Guarabira, Brazil; Mauro Morelli, Auxiliary Bishop

of São Paulo, Brazil; and Alfredo Nowak, Auxiliary Bishop of São Paulo, Brazil.

The sentiments they express in this telegram were also communicated to us by telephone. They told us about the indignation this news caused in the meeting the bishops were having in Brazil and how they felt moved to send the telegram. In responding to this, I want to echo the applause of the people and tell them how gratified we feel at this moment when our voice, which is blocked from the airwaves, needs to find continental support. Perhaps we wouldn't have found such support had our transmitter not been bombed!

Among other expressions of solidarity there stands out this telegram of the Revolutionary Governing Junta:

> We deplore and condemn the dynamite attack which yesterday destroyed the transmitter of YSAX, the PanAmerican Voice, the radio station of the Archdiocese of San Salvador. Through this medium we express to your Excellency, and through you to the Catholic Church of El Salvador, our deep regret regarding this senseless terrorist act directed against an important means of social communication. Sincerely, the Revolutionary Governing Junta.

The people have expressed their views with a wide range of emotions. Some are protesting, as this lovely letter says:

> This radio station speaks for the people. There always are and there always will be Herods and Caiphases who don't want the people to know what they should know. It doesn't suit them! My contribu-

tion is small, but if twenty thousand Catholics decide to help this crusade, which begins right now with these five colones I am sending, then YSAX will quickly be on the air again. And if they destroy it again, we will rebuild again, let them be sure of that!

This wonderful letter concludes with the words: "The people can do it because it is God's cause!"

The gamut of emotions also includes the sorrow and anguish of many. Some are even weeping because the sounds of our station were like members of the family and now they miss them. A beautiful letter from the Committee Promoting a Ministry of Health says this:

> We make you know of our sadness because of the attack on our Catholic radio station, YSAX, which until now has been the voice of the Church and of all the people who are seeking to build a kingdom of peace, justice, and love. But we believe that this attack will not silence the denunciation of the injustices that our people are suffering. We are in solidarity with the sorrow of all Christians who will not have the opportunity to hear the truth that is transmitted to us by our station.

Also, many spontaneous gestures of support have been forthcoming. Yesterday I was in Botoncillal, a village in the parish of Colón, and I admired the spontaneity of a young man who made an appeal to the people to take up a collection. What was collected among those poor campesinos was money, yes, but what was most valuable was the affection with which they made their donations. Yesterday, as we were entering San Salvador and had to stop for a red light, someone shouted to me, "For the station!" When I looked out to see who it was, I saw a taxi driver who had five colones in his hand. This was the voice of the street, the voice of the people who are ready to help our radio station! Some young people also invited me to Sonzacate (with permission of the bishop of Santa Ana), and the people attending the Eucharist there yesterday took up a collection with great spontaneity and affection. They offered it to me as the first fruits of the diocese of Santa Ana.

I want especially to thank the other media. All of them published the bulletin I put out, and some of them have published commentaries protesting the bombing. One of them even had an editorial praising our station.

I also want to thank the technicians of the UCA [the University of Central America], who have offered to restore our station as soon as possible. I have personally assumed responsibility for getting the station running again, and with your tremendous support I am confident that we can set up an YSAX that will be much more powerful than the one they've destroyed.

Right here we can see still another delightful gesture of solidarity: many dear sisters and brothers with their recorders will be bringing this message on cassettes to places the station cannot reach. As long as this silence lasts, these recorders and cassettes will be providing a service!

One thing has surprised me profoundly and made me very grateful. As I entered [the cathedral] for Mass today, a representative of Radio Noticias del Continente, of Costa Rica, told me that he would be recording our celebration so that immediately afterward it can be retransmitted in Costa Rica on the 31-meter shortwave band. So our homily will reach not just the small broadcast area of our station but all of Central America and the entire world, thanks to this shortwave station of Costa Rica, Radio Noticias del Continente. Next Sunday, if we are still in the same situation, this generous Costa Rican radio station is going to transmit the celebration of our Mass directly. When you leave Mass today, if you have a shortwave radio, you can look for the 31-meter band, and you will hear what people around the world will be hearing. Our poor homily will be reaching horizons we never even suspected before the bomb! So you see, sisters and brothers, nobody can destroy the projects of God!

So my third introductory reflection is to urge all of you to take Lent seriously. The essence of our message is, thank God, something that nobody can destroy, and it is more important than any of the technical, material things that the extreme right can damage. And there are many Catholics who possess more technical skill than do those who destroy with bombs. We are concerned about the material aspect because we know the immense good accomplished by the radio. All the same, we say once again that the spoken word is useless if it just vibrates and sounds without incarnating itself in the lives of Christians. Christ's greatest concern is that we Christians be truly a living word, a light for the world, and salt of the earth (Matt 5:13). He wants our communities and our individual lives to bear witness to the Gospel that the Church preaches. Even without radio and technical gear, Christians keep preaching the great liberating message of Christianity far and wide.

I urge you, then, to have an intense experience of this Lent as a journey toward Easter so that, as we celebrate the resurrection, we will be filled with new life and will be the men and women that El Salvador needs in these times. At the end of Lent our Church wants to have the satisfaction of offering to the nation a renewed people and a Church pulsating with the risen Christ. Let us be a Church embracing the cross of the Lord and ready to carry out God's true project for saving our country. This, then, is the theme of our homily.

The title for our reflections will be "Lent Is the Triumph of God's Saving Project in History." God has a project to save history and to save humankind, and Lent reveals to us how this project of God triumphs over the temptations of wickedness. I will present three ideas in today's reflection: the first will be Christ's victory over the enemy of God's saving project; the second will be the action of the Holy Spirit as the force of God's saving project; and the third will be our participation by faith in God's saving project.

Christ's Victory over the Enemy of God's Saving Project

First of all, this Sunday speaks to us about the victory of Christ over the enemy of God's saving project. Today's gospel presents us with the confrontation between two powerful forces: Christ and the devil. Christ presents himself as a man who is going to learn by personal experience the value of temptation for strengthening one's convictions. His journey out into the desert evokes for us the forty years that Israel journeyed in the desert under the guidance of God's project; it reminds us of the temptations, the difficulties, and the adversities they suffered at the hands of the world and the devil. This whole passage evokes the book of Deuteronomy, where Moses spoke to the people, reminding them of the marvels that God had done for them during the Exodus and how he expected the people to remain faithful. It is as though Christ was representing that people during this marvelous stay in the desert: Christ praying, Christ fasting, Christ confronting the temptations of evil. He matured as a man during this testing, and his victory would be so resplendent that during his three years of teaching, these principles by which he overcame the temptations that were seeking to destroy God's project would continue to shine forth.

For the ancients the desert was an uninhabitable area, a place for wild beasts and demons. As Christ entered into that lonely space, he was like a new Adam, but he was not entering into a delightful paradise; rather, his task was to recreate paradise from the desert. He was the second Adam, the redeemer of humankind, transforming the desert into a paradise for us if only we know how to follow his paths.

Then came the temptations: "If you are the Son of God and are hungry, why don't you tell that stone to turn into bread?" Christ answered him, "One does not live by bread alone; rather, every word that comes forth from the mouth of God is for the life of humankind" (Luke 4:3–4). Here two projects can be seen: the project of God and the project of the devil, the project of evil. Let us now observe very carefully in which of these projects we are personally involved. The devil promises Christ an easy solution to the problem: perform a miracle, turn the stones into bread. Such short-term solutions are the kind many politicians want; they want to fix things by doing what is nearly impossible. Their silly attitudes are a lot like the devil's temptation: just turn stones into bread and we are free of hunger!

But God's project wants to give meaning to fasting; it wants to give meaning to the cross, to the desert, to sacrifice. Bread will come soon. The word of God is justice, and bread is not made only from stones. The bread that should nourish all men and women must be the just distribution of goods; it must be the rich giving up what they have to share with the poor; it must be a society ordered according to the heart and the justice of God. "This is the redemption I bring," says Christ. "There is no need to resolve matters easily with miracles, though they are certainly within my reach. Sometimes I will use them," says Christ, "as when I take five loaves of bread to feed five thousand people. For me it is not difficult to multiply loaves and give food and good wages and a good life to all who are forsaken, but we would not fix the world that way. The rich would continue to be selfish, and people would not be converted. We would not form the society that God wants, the society of intelligent people who love one another. With the possessions you have now, you have enough bread for everybody!"

When speaking about artificial methods of birth control, Pope Paul VI said the following: "How sad is the human situation when the banquet of life is denied to some only because we don't know how to share the banquet of life better. It is not a question of denying people entry into life but of preparing the table so that there is bread for all."[3] We could say the same today: let us not seek immediate solutions. Let us not try to organize all at once a society that has been unjustly disorganized for such a long time. But yes, let us organize the conversion of hearts. Let us all learn to experience the austerity of the desert. Let us savor the powerful redemption of the cross. There is no joy greater than earning our bread by the sweat of our brow, and there is no sin more diabolical than taking bread away from those who are hungry.

Today's gospel has another detail about the project of God and the project of evil. It says that the devil then made all the kingdoms and glories of the world pass before Christ in a kind of vision. There were the great parades of troops

---

3. The actual words of Paul VI are these: "Your task is to act in such a manner that there is abundant bread on the table of humanity; it is not to promote birth control, which is irrational since it diminishes the number of guests at the banquet of life." "Message to All Humanity," 27 (Discourse to the General Assembly of the United Nations, October 4, 1965).

and the chariots of emperors. All that was the glory of the world. "All this is mine, and I will give it to you if you fall on your knees and worship me." What pretensions and what sad possessions! I wouldn't want to have anything that came from the devil! So Christ responded to him with God's project: "It is written: 'You shall worship God alone, and him alone shall you serve'" (Luke 4:5–7).

Christ suffered hunger in the desert, but he did not sell out to the idolatry of power. This is a tremendous and timely lesson for our day. Why are people fighting in El Salvador? For power? Doesn't the devil say that power is his and that it's easy to get it, just by kneeling down before him? But the project of God says, "No to idolatry!" In my pastoral letter I state that one of the services the Church is providing today is the unmasking of all idolatries: the idolatry of money, the idolatry of power, and the attempt to get people to kneel before those false gods.[4] The truth is found in God's project: "You shall worship the Lord your God." This is the real solution.

The true liberation of our people comes from teaching them about the struggle that is going on among the false powers of earth, which are mounting constant assaults on human dignity and human rights. They establish political systems that deaden the consciences of the powerful. Woe to the powerful when they discount the power of God, the only powerful One! Woe to them when they torture and kill and massacre in order to subjugate people to power! What terrible sacrifices are being offered to the god of power, the god of money! There are so many victims, so much blood, that God, the true God, the Author of human life, will exact a high price of these worshipers of power!

---

4. "The Church's Mission in the Midst of the Nation's Crisis" (August 6, 1979), 37.

But there is a third vision related by Luke in this gospel. In the third temptation the devil, who never wants to let himself be beaten, carried Christ to the pinnacle of the temple, which is on the corner overlooking the Cedron Valley near Jerusalem. There he presented Christ with another temptation: "Look, throw yourself down from here because it is written: 'God will send his angels to catch you.' After that feat the crowds in the temple will hail you, and you will be the Messiah that this people is expecting and praying for." Responding to this temptation, Christ cited the project of God: "It is also written: 'You shall not tempt the Lord your God.' You want to test me to see whether I am a vain Messiah seeking applause from the people, winning the crowds over by providing them simple solutions and displaying myself as glorious before them. That is not the project of God!" (Luke 4:9–12). The project of God is to be found in the simplicity of those who live their ordinary lives with faith and so win the good will of God and cling to him.

There is no need to perform ostentatious deeds. There is no need for triumphalist religion or triumphalist politics—indeed, they can do much harm. What is needed is more honest simplicity and solid dedication to the service of God. The project of God consists in giving our simple, ordinary lives a spirit of freedom and love. How beautiful our country would be if we all lived according to this project of God! We would all work at our jobs without trying to dominate anybody. We would be justly earning the bread our family needs, and eating it! There would be none of this terrible situation that now arises because people are seeking a false messiah, like the one Satan proposed.

Christ triumphed over the projects of evil and clung to the authentic project that embodied God's ideal, and that is what all Christians must do. Jesus overcame the temptations in the name of all men and women. I am there with him also, and so is each one of you. We must learn how the project of evil can enter into us: for some it will be by pride, for others by greed, for others by vanity, and for others by easy victories. Take great care, sisters and brothers. Christ today has spoken words that must be on the lips of each one of us as we face the cunning temptations of life. We must be brave in defending the only project that saves and endures: the project of God!

The way of the cross is the only path that leads to true victory, and who doesn't carry the cross? Trying to get rid of the cross is to give in to the temptation of the devil. Embracing with affection the cross of my duty—that is the project of God! Lovingly living your own lives—that is how God wants to save humankind!

Christ now appears victorious, but I ask you not to forget during Lent this marvelous figure of Christ in the desert. He is surrounded by wild animals and tempted by the devil, but he is also recovering paradise. And he will recover it decisively when all men and women are, like him, faithful followers of the project of God.

The Action of the Holy Spirit as the Force of God's Saving Project

My second reflection concerns the action of the Holy Spirit as the force of God's saving project. How insistently the Gospel of Saint Luke tells us that Christ was "driven by the Spirit" (Luke 4:1)! That is why the Gospel of Saint Luke is called "the Gospel of the Spirit." Christ was conceived as the Savior of humankind under the impulse of the Spirit of God, beginning even when he was in the womb of the Virgin Mary. The Holy Spirit was the origin of the human nature that was intimately united with the divine person of God the Son. From that time on Christ was the work of the Holy Spirit, and all his work of redemption was the work of the Holy Spirit. We have to be very mindful of this in order to understand the other readings today.

The first reading is the creed of the people of Israel. Let us keep it in mind because the God in which they believed was not a disincarnate God but the God of history. Thus, when the citizens of Israel were harvesting their fields, Moses commanded them to take the first fruits to the temple and to offer them to God with that great prayer which is Israel's creed: "You shall declare before the Lord, your God, 'My father was a wandering Aramean who went down to Egypt and lived there with a small household. Then he became a nation great, strong, and numerous. When the Egyptians maltreated and oppressed us, imposing hard labor upon us, we cried to the Lord, the God of our fathers. The Lord heard our cry and saw our oppression'" (Deut 26:47). The passage then describes how God delivered them from Egypt, led them through the desert, and gave them a country, a Promised Land.

Israel's creed is pure history. It begins with the incredible promise to the patriarchs. An old man who was sterile and had no children was promised a great many descendants. A people that had multiplied under slavery was told by God that they would be given a land "flowing with milk and honey." That people set out for the Promised Land, and when it became a reality, the fruits that it yielded were the proof that God had kept his promise. The fruits were offered in Israel in a sort of "Mass," like our offertory, to give thanks for the land and the country and to commemorate God's faithfulness to his people.

This is a truly fine creed. It explains why the faith of Israelites was not something ethereal, as is that of many Christians today who believe that when the Church talks about these things she is meddling in politics. The faith of Israel was faith in their politics; it was faith and politics converted into a single act of love for the Lord; it was politics inspired by the graces and promises of God. And that is how the God of all people and the God of El Salvador must be: he sheds light on our politics. He is the one who gives us our fields; he is the one who wants agrarian reform; he is the one who wants a more just sharing of the goods that El Salvador produces. It is not just for a few to accumulate wealth in their coffers while the people are left without any of the gifts that God has given for his people.

The creed of Israel was inspired by the Holy Spirit, that same Spirit who gives unity to the whole of Israel's history. That is why the Bible, which is the history of that people, appears as the book of the Holy Spirit. Although it was written by people of diverse cultures and diverse centuries, it was the Holy Spirit who was writing the pages of Israel's history. The Bible, then, is a model for all the histories of all the world's peoples. Everyone must therefore read the Bible and learn from it the relationship between faith and politics. The Bible is an instruction book that teaches us how to experience that marvelous relationship between faith and politics.

Accordingly, the Holy Spirit led the history of Israel toward its fullness, which came with the birth of Christ by the Holy Spirit. At that moment Christ began to form for himself a new Christian people, and that is who we are. We the people rise up again for we are the work of the Holy Spirit. God continues the history of salvation in the history of every people, and no empire should come and interfere with our people's way of being. The God of the great empires is demanding justice of the powerful and defending the poor of the people. He already has plenty to do there! The God of our impoverished peoples is continuing the history of salvation with our Salvadoran history, not with fabricated histories.

The history inspired by the Holy Spirit gives the Christian people the marvelous incentive of the resurrection. The Spirit who raised up Christ has given us the model for history in the risen Christ. It is in that direction that every history must tend, toward creating men and women who, after carrying the cross all their lives, receive the new life of freedom. We should enjoy freedom also on earth, but its fullness we will enjoy only in the kingdom of God. That doesn't mean that we're going to leave the people's liberation for the other side of death. What I am saying is that the risen Christ already belongs to our present history; he is the fount of human freedom and dignity. That is precisely why we celebrate Lent as preparation for Easter. After experiencing the Lent which is our Salvadoran situation, we will enjoy the new life of the risen Christ as we seek a more just and harmonious country, one where people will live with intensity the life of God that Christ brings with him and gives us through his paschal mystery.

Therefore, Lent and Easter are our own reality, and every people can say the same thing. And Christ is ours; Christ is Salvadoran for us Salvadorans. Christ has risen for us, here in El Salvador. And our history will be a history of resurrection and freedom and dignity in the measure that we allow ourselves to be led by the Spirit who led Jesus. Let us search, by the force of the Spirit, for our own special character, our own history, our own freedom, our own dignity as a Salvadoran people.

Our Participation by Faith in the Victory of God's Saving Project

Finally, the third reflection of this homily is that we participate by faith in the victory of God's saving project. Today's first reading, as I told you, contains the profession of faith of the people of Israel, which consists mainly of the three great articles of Israelite faith. First, the calling of the patriarchs. God chose Abraham, an Aramean without special merit, and made of him a great people, starting almost from nothing. The second article of the Israelite creed professes that God made a people and delivered them from slavery to independence, from Egypt to Exodus. And the third part of the creed of Israel says that, just as God made a people, we have to continue to make this people according to the heart of God. This Israelite creed changes for Christians but without betraying its origins.

Today's second reading helps us to understand better the divine aspect of our history. Saint Paul gives us a marvelous description today of both the process and the content of Christian faith. The process is quite simple, says Saint Paul. "The word is near you. You have it on your lips and in your heart" (Rom 10:8). This is the first thing: proclaiming the word of God and bringing it closer to people. This is the mission of the preacher, and this is the mission of the radio. That is why we miss it, and we must have it again one day. The carriers of the word bring the word closer to the people. Saint Paul says that faith begins when people feel the word close by. "How can they believe if they have not heard?" he asks (Rom 10:14). We must first hear in order to believe or not believe, but first comes hearing, when the word comes near. What a great mission we have in this process of faith, dear sisters and brothers, parents, catechists, teachers in our Christian schools! Ours is the mission of bringing God's word closer to the ears of the people.

After the word is heard, it is received in the heart; faith is accepted and interiorized: "I believe." But the interior reception of faith is not enough, says Saint Paul. It must be made explicit; it must be externalized, and that happens through the liturgical signs. The sacraments are the signs of the faith that we carry in our hearts and so are called the "sacraments of faith." That is why people should not receive a sacrament if they don't know what they are receiving. It's for that reason that we are insisting that children should not be baptized until the meaning of baptism has been explained to the parents and godparents. Similarly, no one should be married by the Church without receiving an explanation of what the sacrament of matrimony means. People should not receive a sacrament unless it is an outward expression of the faith they carry within them.

The sacraments should proceed from faith. Coming to Mass on Sunday is a sacrament. The Eucharist brings us together because we believe that Christ is present as our leader guiding us on this pilgrimage. We come every Sunday, filled with faith, in order to feel more united with him. We are manifesting our faith. Those who are not Catholic do not attend Mass because it is not part of their faith, but when we come to Mass, we are saying, "Today I am going to holy Mass to share this interior faith I have with my sisters and brothers." As I was telling you before, we must become the microphones of God. This faith we have can be transmitted by our good example, by our honesty, by our friendly words, by the consolation we offer others. We should be models of the word of God that is fully alive in the depths of our being. That is faith!

What is the content of this Christian faith? Saint Paul tells us two things today: believe that Christ is the Lord, and believe that God has raised him from the dead (Rom 10:9). Those are the two great articles of Christian faith. First, that Christ is the Lord. Saying "Lord" means saying "God." Only before Christ are we to bend our knees. Only Christ are we to seek, and never should we accept anything else in place of Christ our Lord. Second, that he rose and now is alive and waiting for us. We believe in a man who died but who is now alive, and death has no dominion over him. This is Christian faith. That is why Lent will prepare us for Easter, when we will be able to say not only with our lips but with our lives, "Christ is the Lord. We don't have to worship anyone else. We bend our knees only before him. Even if we die, we will die always kneeling before Christ! Never will we find life kneeling before humans!"

As you can see, dear sisters and brothers, the contents of the faith of the New Testament are a little different from those of the Old Testament, but the meaning and the spirit of the faith are the same. When Israelites professed their faith, they said, "We believe in the God who chose Abraham. We believe in the God who formed a people and delivered them from Egypt. We believe in the God who gave us this land with all its fruits." What they were saying was this: "We trust in God. We believe in him. We dedicate ourselves to him and adore no other god." Now Christians say, "We believe that Christ is the Lord. We believe that Christ rose and is now alive." The contents are different, but the object is the same: we must believe in God; we must worship God; we must follow Christ. For the Israelites, Christ did not yet exist; they had only the promise that God was to become human. For us Christians, that great promise of history is now reality. Christ is God become man. For us, the whole history of Israel is changed by our belief in the One who personifies Israel. Christ is the personification of all that long history of salvation. Lent prepares us to be worthy to follow the true Christ.

So the conclusion is this, sisters and brothers: let us have faith. Let us truly believe, and with our faith let us shed light on our politics, let us work at history, let us fashion the destiny of our people. But let us not make a project that is merely human, much less one inspired by the devil. Let us make a project that is inspired by God and that leads us to believe in Christ. Let us make a project that helps us realize that the history of our country is a history of salvation because Christ is involved with our families, with the laws of our country, with our government, and with everything else that has to do with our country. Let Christ be the light that shines everywhere so that our country will become the entryway to that great kingdom of God.

[Romero continued as usual with his section on the "Life of the Church," this week emphasizing his gratitude for the many words and gestures of solidarity from around the country and the world.]

Events of the Week

Finally, sisters and brothers, I want to consider the country's politics from the Church's viewpoint. I do this not as a politician, for I am not one, but as a pastor guiding his people by the light of Christian principles. Since all of you experience these political realities in your lives, and I also experience them as pastor, we must know how to judge them and criticize them by Gospel standards, and we must learn how to collaborate and commit ourselves to making our history conform to the project of God.

. . .

Our Legal Aid Office has been giving us some very sad information these days. This week many bodies with evident signs of torture were found in different parts of the country. There has been an average of six unidentified bodies a day, some of them marked with the initials of the criminal gangs of the extreme right. On February 20 in Mejicanos, for example, two bodies were thrown from a moving vehicle, one about thirty-six years old and the other about twenty-eight; they had been tortured and their throats were cut. On February 19 some individuals opened fire on the church in Tonacatepeque and killed six persons who were in the town park. So far in the month of February at least fifty *campesinos* in Aguilares have been tortured, shot, and killed. At noon on February 21 two employees of the Office for Poor Assistance, Doctor José Antonio Baires Zelaya and Ricardo Alfredo Torres, were brutally killed, and two law students were also wounded.

The terrible murder of Doctor Mario Zamora has been reported, and the Christian Democratic Party has offered this reflection on it:

The Party, speaking to the national conscience, holds responsible for this appalling crime Major Roberto D'Aubuisson[5] and the band of assassins commanded by the extreme right. The connection is clear between the denunciation made on television by this sinister individual and the criminal act that obliterated the valiant life of this man dedicated to serving

---

5. Roberto D'Aubuisson was a symbol of the unity of the military and the right-wing death squads in the country. He is believed to have been the architect of the plot to kill Romero. In the years after Romero's death, he would lead the conservative ARENA party. Mario Zamora Rivas, leader of the Christian Democratic Party and director of the Office of Services for the Poor, was killed on February 23, 1980. On a television program three days earlier, Roberto D'Aubuisson had accused him of belonging to a guerrilla group, the People's Liberation Forces (FPL). The quotations in the homily come from *La Prensa Gráfica* (February 24, 1980) and *El Independiente* (February 26, 1980).

the most noble and generous efforts to help the Salvadoran people. The Party thus repeats its repudiation of the violence which is causing bloodshed in our anguished country.

I want to express my own personal sorrow to the family of our dear Doctor Mario Zamora Rivas. At this time his body is being interred in Cojutepeque. Let us join together in prayer for his eternal rest.

On February 21 in Suchitoto known members of ORDEN ambushed the *campesinos* Jeremías Melgar and Osmaro Acosta and killed both of them. Osmar was a close relative of Lucio Elías Acosta, who was killed in similar circumstances on February 13. Also on February 21, in the village of Amayo in Aguilares, members of ORDEN, with the protection of security forces, killed the *campesinos* Teodoro Vega, Miguel Ángel Rivas Ruiz, Manuel Marroquín, and Carlos Alvarado.

Still another teacher was killed, José Abilio Torres Benavides. So far this year, nine teachers have been killed. In a spirit of friendship I also want to join in the sorrow of the family of Edgar Béneke, another victim of this wave of violence in our country.

. . .

Since we are now in the season of Lent, which is a time for conversion and reflection on what it means to be Christian, I want to make a fraternal, pastoral appeal to the oligarchy. I ask you to be converted to life and to use your economic power for the people's benefit instead of for the misery and ruin of our population. If you don't want to listen to me, then at least listen to the voice of Pope John Paul II. This very week, at the beginning of Lent, he exhorted the Catholics of the world to give up superfluous wealth in order to help the needy and to do this as a sign of Lenten penance.[6]

In this regard I want to recall what Pope Paul VI said about there being two ways of celebrating Lent: one way for the economically developed countries, and another way for the poor countries where Lent is perpetual because they are always fasting. In the former, Lent should consist of giving up something and promoting the value of austerity, while in the latter Lent is different. Among our own people, who constantly suffer hunger and privation, understanding their situation in a penitential sense doesn't mean accepting it passively. Lent should mean working so that social justice will prevail in the country. The best way for us to celebrate Lent will be to work for social justice out of love for the poor, as Pope John Paul II told me to do during my visit to Rome.

The same pontiff has stated that the goods that for some people are superfluous are an essential requirement for the survival of hundreds of millions of human beings. The pope also stressed an essential point of the Christian message when he said that the Church is not interested simply in there being a more equitable distribution of wealth. She wants that distribution to result from a true desire among all human beings to share not only material goods but life itself with those who are disadvantaged in our society. This is something wonderful. Social justice is not just a law demanding distribution; seen from a Christian viewpoint, it is an interior attitude, like that of Christ who, being rich, became poor in order to be able to share his love with the poor (2 Cor 8:9).

---

6. John Paul II, "Message of the Holy Father to the People of God at the Beginning of Lent," February 19, 1980, in *L'Osservatore Romano* (February 24, 1980).

I hope that this appeal to them from the Church doesn't harden even more the hearts of the oligarchs but instead moves them to conversion. You must share who you are and what you have. Don't keep silencing with violence those of us who extend to you this invitation. More importantly, don't keep killing those of us who are trying to achieve a more just distribution of the power and the wealth of our country. I speak in the first person because this week I was advised that I am on the list of those they are planning to eliminate next week. But let it be shown that the voice of justice cannot be killed by anybody.

For this reason I think that this call to conversion extends also to the armed forces. At the beginning of this year the supreme authorities of this institution promised to support a process of reform that was anti-oligarchic and for the benefit of the people. It is now time, especially during Lent when we hear the urgent appeals of the Gospel, for them to honor this commitment if they wish to be true to their military pledge. Don't let the oligarchy continue to use you to defend their interests! Guarantee freedom of expression, of movement, of organization, and the rest. Support the efforts to bring about the authentic changes the country requires.

It appears that the United States State Department is conditioning its economic and military aid on the government's willingness to carry the reforms into practice. As I said last Sunday, it is evident that until now that condition has not been fulfilled. A recent press notice, however, stated the following: "The United States today warned the conservative military leaders of El Salvador that Washington's relations with that country would be damaged if the armed forces were to block the reform program of the moderate government that now holds power.... We do not want United States aid to El Salvador to contribute to repression in that country or to be used to frustrate reforms."[7] The reporter referred to the letter I read to you last Sunday, which one member of the United States government described as "devastating." I did not mean to devastate anything but simply to ask in the name of the people that the military aid not be unconditional. Now, thank God, it seems that the eyes of the United States have been opened so that the aid will be strictly monitored and not result in evil and in the repression of our people. And this is necessary because the stance of the armed forces has become ever more pro-oligarchy and more brutally repressive.

Speaking with words of the Gospel and calling all to conversion, I earnestly desire that the United States provide no more aid until our armed forces are converted. Moreover, I continue to ask, no matter what happens, that no part of that aid be used for training or equipping the armed forces, for they offer no guarantee of remaining faithful to the people for long. Finally, I want to reaffirm my desire that no American economic aid given to the Salvadoran people should place limits on their legitimate right to self-determination. As long as there is no guarantee that this right will be respected and that none of the aid will be used to continue repressing the people, there is no justice or benefit for the country in any aid, no matter what country it comes from.

My Lenten appeal for the conversion of the diverse sectors of Salvadoran society would not be complete if I did not, as pastor, address an affectionate message to the grassroots forces. There is an urgent need for the people's organizations to continue maturing so that they can carry out their mission of being interpreters of the will of the people. Given the

---

7. "Conditions Placed on United States Aid to El Salvador" in *La Prensa Gráfica* (February 23, 1980).

great dignity of our people, their suffering and oppression should not be manipulated; rather, it should be guided by a true spirituality of poverty, as we recalled last Sunday. Their poverty is a denunciation of the injustice of our country, but it is also a spirituality. The poor have in their hands a great instrument for being holy and pleasing to God. Poverty means being as dedicated as Christ was, for he, though being rich, chose to live with the poor to save them, and to do so precisely by his poverty. I praise here the efforts of all those Christians who make this generous commitment to the sacrifice of poverty.

In calling the poor and the organizations to conversion, I want to cite these wise words of a beloved Salvadoran writer:

> If those of us who, being poor, have no economic interests to defend and have suffered no personal harm, nevertheless feel intense desires for severe judgment against those who have altered the peace and destroyed the national economy, then how much greater must be the wrath and the violent reaction of those who have seen their possessions destroyed and great damage done to countless poor families? To the oligarchs can be applied the words of the book of Wisdom which say, "Terribly and swiftly shall come upon you the wrath of God. The mighty shall be mightily tested" (Wis 6:5–6). But is it with proletarian terrorist violence that the repressive violence of millionaires should be and can be combated? Our people are left with no other alternative than violence—so think even some Catholics who say they're progressive. Second, is it with bombs, arson, occupations, kidnappings, and even murders that the kingdom of God and its jus-

tice will in the end be established? Third, do you believe that it is the Holy Spirit rather than the devil that
is inspiring these acts of vandalism which harm Christian moral life more than they harm the estates of the
oligarchs? To defend or cover up subversive violence,
instead of condemning it outright, will in my opinion
only provoke more repressive insolence, for we are
seeing on all sides the reaction of the bloodthirsty
forces of repression against any attack of the groups
of subversion.[8]

It seems to me, then, that during this Lent we have to try
to achieve a sane balance.[9] I repeat that the Church has defended and will continue to defend the right to organize and
all just demands. The Church believes in the role that the people's organizations can play as political forces. At the same
time, the Church calls them to continue to grow so that they
become a true expression of a people that is not violent by nature but rather loves peace and seeks reasonable solutions.

. . .

Sisters and brothers, the history of our people is very
complex and weighty, but I am consoled by knowing that it
is being illuminated by the history of salvation. Today Christ
in the desert has taught us that people can be influenced either by the law of God's project or by temptations to evil.
That Christ, who is the Son of Man because he represents all
human beings, has a great message for us this Sunday. We

---

8. The author of this quotation is unknown.

9. Recall that this was his central point in the second homily in this
book, at the "One Mass" on March 20, 1977.

are working out our history under two influences: our Christian faith and the evil forces of crime, violence, and other vices that are right now dictating our history.

Like Jesus in the desert, I ask you to reflect especially on what God's project is. As Christians, each and every one of us should be a reflection of that project of God. Before anything else we should seek the will of the Lord and not follow the caprices of human beings, especially when these are inspired by crimes of selfishness. Let us seek for what God wants, even in the hunger of the desert, even on the cross of his own Son. God wants to save the world not just by appearances but by the true force that emanates solely from the cross and from sacrifice. So Lent summons all of us to love our homeland but also to enlighten it regarding the path by which the Lord wants to lead it so that we are not left disillusioned. In our Mass today, then, we are going forth like the Israelites to proclaim our faith in the God of our history.

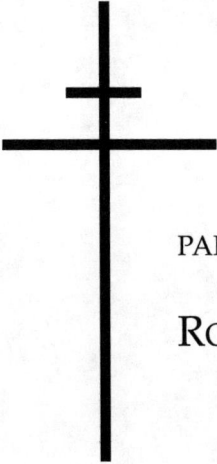

PART VI

ROMERO'S FINAL WORDS

The Church Serves Personal, Communal, and Transcendent Liberation

(March 23, 1980)

R omero's most famous and most quoted words come at the conclusion of the long Sunday homily he gave on March 23, 1980:

> I would like to make an appeal especially to the men of the army, and concretely to the National Guard, the police, and the troops. Brothers, you are a part of our own people. You are killing your own brother and sister *campesinos*, and against any order a man may give to kill, God's law must prevail: "You shall not kill!" (Exod 20:13). No soldier is obliged to obey an order against the law of God. No one has to observe an immoral law. It is time now for you to reclaim your conscience and to obey your conscience rather than the command to sin. The Church defends the rights of God, the law of God, and the dignity of the human person and therefore cannot remain silent before such great abominations. We want the government to understand well that the reforms are worth nothing if they are

stained with so much blood. In the name of God, then, and in the name of this suffering people, whose laments rise up each day more tumultuously toward heaven, I beg you, I beseech you, I order you in the name of God: Stop the repression!

These words were not a homiletic aside nor a spur-of-the moment decision. They were long-prepared and carefully discerned. Romero preached for over an hour and forty minutes that Sunday. In some ways, Romero's whole homily was a long build-up to the culminating moment.

Yet even the night before, Romero was pondering these precise words. As he sat with the head of his legal aid office to discuss the documented cases of violence and oppression that week, he asked for his friend's legal and personal opinion on whether he should proclaim these words the next day. His friend told him that the appeal to soldiers to disobey orders probably violated Salvadoran law, but that it was his decision. Romero then spent most of the night in prayer in his chapel, seeking strength and guidance.

And really, all of Lent was a preparation for this decisive moment. Romero's preaching in March of 1980 responded to the increasingly desperate situation of the country and urgently called for conversion among all factions. He urged the country to truly enter into this season of preparation and penitence as a recommitment to the project of God and the dignity of every person. A selection of passages draws together well his message:

Since Lent prepares us to celebrate the feast of our redemption, our observance of Lent cannot disregard the concrete circumstances in which Christians and others celebrate this very meaningful season.... Lent should awaken in us a sense of social justice. (March 2, 1980)

The Church must always keep the human person in sight. This is the star that guides her along the way. She is often misunderstood and often maligned because many people want to make their earthly projects prevail. All the Church is concerned about is the human being, the child of God, and that is why she grieves over all human corpses being found, over the torture of human beings, over the suffering of human beings. For the Church the goal of all projects must be this great project of God: the human being. Every person is a child of God, and in every person killed the Church venerates a sacrificed Christ. (March 2, 1980)

Luke's Gospel teaches us to ask ourselves: What use is our life, as pompous as it may appear, if it produces no fruit? We are barren fig trees! The Gospel also tells us that God is waiting for us with gentleness and patience. Lent is urgently calling us to review our lives in order to see whether we really are bearing fruits or are simply useless fig trees taking up space in the world. There is a great need today for active, critical Christians who do not accept social conditions without analyzing them internally and profoundly. Today we don't want masses of people who let themselves be easily controlled, as has been the case for so long. We want men and women who, like fruit-producing fig

234 ROMERO'S FINAL WORDS

trees, can say yes to justice and no to injustice.
(March 9, 1980)

God has taught us that he is a God who wants to be
with humanity. He is a God who feels the pain of
those who are tortured and die in agony. He is a
God who, with the Church, denounces torture, repression, and all such crimes. The God we adore is
not a dead God; he is a living God who feels, acts,
labors, and leads this history forward. In him we
hope, in him we trust. God walks with us, as he
walked with Israel. (March 9, 1980)

How providential this Lenten message is, sisters
and brothers, in its call to conversion! And we are
especially called to reconciliation in our present situation, where reconciliation is truly more needed
than ever. There is tremendous violence, tremendous hatred, tremendous selfishness. Everyone
thinks they have the truth; everyone blames others
for all the evils. We have become "polarized" —
that's the word being used to describe the reality
we're experiencing. Without being aware of it, we
have become individually polarized, bound to a
pole of fixed ideas, incapable of reconciliation,
filled with mortal hatred. That is not the reality
God wants. As never before, our society is in need
of God's great love and great reconciliation. As pastor I invite you to hear my words, sisters and brothers; they are only a rough, imperfect echo, but don't
mind the instrument. Take heed of what the infinite
love of God commands: Be converted! Be reconciled! Love one another! Become a people of the

baptized, a family of God's children! (March 16, 1980).

This message rang out from the cathedral and across the whole country each Sunday in Lent.

But we must look even farther back to understand Romero's most famous words from Sunday, March 23. As early as January 1980, we see Romero lamenting the military violence; he also received letters from soldiers seeking his guidance. In the name of national security and of fighting Marxism, they were being ordered to attack rural villages and kill innocent civilians indiscriminately. They begged Romero for help. As soldiers, they had pledged obedience to their superiors, but these were orders they knew they shouldn't obey. Romero's famous words were, in part, an answer to these letters.

Ultimately, however, we can see Romero's whole ministry as leading up to this moment. His opening appeal to the armed forces—"Brothers, you are a part of our own people"—had been his message for three years. Romero had tried for three years to help his people see and judge the world around them in the light of the Gospel. He had pleaded for his people to see one another truly as brothers and sisters, to help build a society of justice and peace that conformed to the project of God.

In his final Sunday homily, Romero explains this project of God as a project of liberation with personal, communal, and transcendent dimensions. Short selections from each part of the homily appear below, with the final, culminating moment given again in full.

Suggestions for Further Reading

Many of the previous homilies provided or recommended in this book anticipate the core themes of Romero's final Sunday homily. Indeed, nearly every homily he preached in some way touches upon the themes of liberation and salvation at the center of his message on March 23, 1980. Nevertheless, I would recommend two earlier homilies as particularly important.

- "Jesus is the True Messiah" (September 16, 1979) in *A Prophetic Bishop Speaks to His People: The Complete Homilies of Archbishop Óscar Arnulfo Romero*, 6 vols., trans. Joseph Owens, SJ (Convivium Press, 2015–2016), 5.296–19.

- "The Three Conditions for Entering the Kingdom of God" (October 14, 1979) in *A Prophetic Bishop Speaks*, 5.383–403.

Sunday, March 23, 1980
Mass Readings
Isaiah 43:16–21; Philippians 3:8–14
John 8:1–11

Just as Christ will flourish in the unending resurrection of Easter, so we must accompany him also in the cross, the sacrifice, and the martyrdom of Lent and Holy Week. He told us, "Blessed are those who are not scandalized by the cross!" Lent, then, is a call to celebrate our redemption in that difficult mystery of cross and victory. At the present time our people are well prepared: all our surroundings speak to us of the cross. But those who have Christian faith and hope know that behind the calvary of El Salvador lies our Easter and our resurrection, and that is the hope we have as a Christian people.

During these Sundays of Lent I have been trying to uncover in divine revelation, in the word read here at Mass, God's project for saving persons and peoples. In our time, when so many diverse historical projects arise for our people, we can be sure that the project that wins out will be the one that best reflects God's project, and this is the Church's mission. It is for this reason, dear sisters and brothers, that we have the duty to examine our own reality in the light of the divine word that reveals God's project. We must try to see whether that project of God is being realized among us or is instead being reviled. No one should take it amiss that we illuminate our social, political, and economic realities by the light of the divine word read in our Mass, because if we did not do so, we would not really be Christian. This is why Christ wanted to become incarnate: so the light that he brings from the Father can become the life of persons and peoples.

I am well aware that many are scandalized by such speech and claim that it's meddling in politics instead of preaching the Gospel, but I don't accept that accusation. I am making an effort to communicate everything taught by the Second Vatican Council and the bishops' meetings at Medellín and Puebla. I do this so that we don't just have it on paper and study it theoretically but rather make it reality and apply it to our situation of conflict. This is how the Gospel must be preached for our people. That is why, as I listen all during the week to the cries of the people and behold so much horrible crime and such shameful violence, I ask the Lord to give me appropriate words for consoling, for denouncing, and for calling to repentance. Though I continue to be a voice crying out in the desert, I know that the Church is trying hard to fulfill her mission.

During these Sundays of Lent, then, we have seen how God's project can be synthesized. Christ is the way, and so he is presented to us as fasting and overcoming temptations in the desert. Christ is the goal and the impulse of life, and so he is presented to us transfigured, thus calling us to that goal to which all men and women are called. Then the Third, Fourth, and Fifth Sundays of Lent explained the collaboration that God asks of us in order to save us, namely, our conversion and reconciliation with him. Some wonderful examples are offered, such as the barren fig tree, the prodigal son, and—this morning—the adulterous woman who repents and is pardoned. God issues his call and tells us that he will treat us in the same way as the father treated the prodigal son and as the Savior treated the adulterous woman. There is no sin that cannot be forgiven, and there is no enmity that cannot be reconciled when there is conversion and sincere return to the Lord. That is the message of Lent!

. . .

In the light of the divine word of today, I am going to present this reflection under the title: "The Church Serves Personal, Communal, and Transcendent Liberation." These three adjectives mark out the three reflections of today's homily: first, there is an urgent need to liberate personal dignity; second, God wants to save the people as a whole; and third, transcendence is the true and definitive dimension of liberation. All this becomes evident from today's readings.

. . .

Personal sin is at the base of the great social sin. We must keep this in mind, dear sisters and brothers, because today it is very easy for us to be like those who witnessed the adultery: we point it out and demand justice, but we look very little into our own consciences. How easy we find it to condemn structural injustice, institutional violence, and social sin! All that is quite real, but where are the sources of that social sin? They are in the heart of every person. Modern-day society is an anonymous society in which nobody accepts blame but everybody is responsible. All of us are responsible for what happens, but the sin remains anonymous. We are all sinners, and we have all contributed our grain of sand to this mountain of crimes and violence in our country.

That is why salvation begins with the human person, with human dignity, with freeing every individual from sin. This is

God's call during Lent: Let each and every one be converted! Among all of us who are here, there are not two sinners who are the same. Each of us has committed our own shameful deeds, but we want to hide them and shift the blame to others. I also am a sinner and must take off my mask. I have offended God and society, and I must ask forgiveness of God. This is the call of Christ: the human person comes first.

. . .

The great task of Christians is to become absorbed in God's kingdom and, with our souls so absorbed, to work also on the projects of history. It is a good thing to unite in the people's organizations; it is a good thing to create political parties; it is a good thing to take part in government. All that is good, as long as you're a Christian who reflects the kingdom of God and tries to implant it wherever you're working—as long as you're not a plaything of earthly ambitions. This is the great duty of today's men and women. I have always told you, dear Christians, and I'll tell you again: it is from here, from Christian groups, from the people of God that the true liberators of our people must emerge. Any historical project not founded on the themes we treated in our first point—the dignity of the human person, the will of God, the kingdom of Christ among us—will be an ephemeral affair. In contrast, the project that best reflects the eternal design of God will be ever more stable and ever more capable of working for the common good of all peoples according to their needs. I ask you, my dear brothers and sisters in politics, not to manipulate the Church so that she will say what you want her to say. Rather, announce what the Church is teaching, for she has no vested interests. I have no desire for power, and that is why I am completely free to tell power what is good and what is bad. I can tell any political group what is good and what is bad—that is my duty.

...

Finally, the third reflection taken from today's readings is that God's project for the liberation of the people is something transcendent. Transcendence is the true and definitive dimension of liberation. I think I may be repeating this idea too much, but I don't tire of repeating it because we are in great danger of wanting to escape from urgent problems by applying immediate solutions, and we forget that short-term measures can be patches and not true solutions. The true solution has to match up with the definitive project of God. Any solution we devise for a better distribution of land, for better financial administration in El Salvador, or for political organizations dedicated to the welfare of Salvadorans will always have to be sought in conjunction with our definitive liberation.

...

Now, then, I invite you to look at our situation from the perspective of this Church which is trying to be the kingdom of God on earth and which therefore must shed light on the realities around us. We have lived through a tremendously tragic week.

...

We continue to review this week that was so loaded with events that must be recounted. News items about the pope say that he also was reporting on the number of victims that there have been these days in Italy and especially in Rome.

That means that if the pope were in my place, not only would he point out the ten cruel murders in Italy, but he would take time, as we are doing now, to recount day by day the numerous killings here.

. . .

Dear sisters and brothers, I don't want to take advantage of your time, but it would be interesting to analyze now the meaning of what has happened during these first few months of a new government which was supposed to deliver us from these horrible situations. If their intention is to decapitate the people's organizations and to thwart the process that the people want, then no other process can move forward. Without sinking roots into the people, no government can be effective, especially if it wants to impose itself through bloodshed and pain.

I would like to make an appeal especially to the men of the army, and concretely to the National Guard, the police, and the troops. Brothers, you are a part of our own people. You are killing your own brother and sister *campesinos*, and against any order a man may give to kill, God's law must prevail: "You shall not kill!" (Exod 20:13). No soldier is obliged to obey an order against the law of God. No one has to observe an immoral law. It is time now for you to reclaim your conscience and to obey your conscience rather than the command to sin. The Church defends the rights of God, the law of God, and the dignity of the human person and therefore cannot remain silent before such great abominations. We want the government to understand well that the reforms are worth nothing if they are stained with so much blood. In the name of God, then, and in the name of this suffering people, whose laments rise up each day more tumultuously toward heaven, I beg you, I beseech you, I order you in the name of God: Stop the repression!

The liberation the Church preaches is just as we have studied it today in the holy Bible. It is a liberation that respects above all the dignity of the person, the saving power of the common good of the people, and the transcendent vision that looks first of all toward God and derives its hope and its strength from God alone. Let us now proclaim our faith in this truth.

The Final Homily of Archbishop Romero

(March 24, 1980)

R omero's appeal to the armed forces of the country
sealed his fate. His call to soldiers to "Stop the repression!" and to disobey immoral orders was too much for the
military to take. An assassination plot that had been conceived months earlier was now quickly put into action.

Romero also knew the dangers when he spoke those
words. His name had appeared on lists of people to be eliminated. Roberto D'Aubuisson, leader of many paramilitary
death squads roaming the country, had publicly criticized
him — an act that often preceded an assassination or disap-
pearance. Romero received an offer from the archbishop of
Panama, Marcos McGrath, to come to Panama for a short
while to ensure his safety. Romero refused. Yet, we should
not imagine Romero in that serenity and indifference in
which saints are often depicted as they go to their death.
Romero was certainly courageous and resolute, but he was
also afraid.

Just weeks earlier, Romero had gone on his annual retreat with several priests of the archdiocese. There he spoke
of his fear of a violent death. He was afraid of what the
coming weeks might bring. As Romero's confessor later

wrote, "I dare to consider this last retreat of his as his prayer in the garden.... Archbishop Romero foresaw his very probable and imminent death. He felt terror at it as Jesus did in the garden. But he did not leave his post and his duty, ready to drink the chalice that the Father might give him to drink."[1] Romero left the retreat with a firm resolve, trusting that, as God had accompanied the martyrs, God would not abandon him. Yet the fear remained. He began to sleep in the old spare room next to the sacristy in the chapel of the hospice center where he lived. He spoke of his fear of a kidnapping or bombing in the night. He slept poorly. He began to drive his car himself, fearing that an attack on him would take the life of his driver as well.

On Monday evening, March 24, Romero celebrated a simple Mass at the chapel of the hospice center. The Mass marked the one-year anniversary of the death of Sara Meardi de Pinto, the mother of the Jorge Pinto, Romero's friend and the editor of the newspaper *El Independiente*. The gospel reading that day was a fitting remembrance for Doña Sarita, but also encapsulated the path taken by Romero himself: "I tell you, unless a grain of wheat falls into the earth and dies, it remains just a single grain, but if it dies it bears much fruit. Those who love their life lose it, and those who hate their life in this world will keep it for eternal life" (John 12:24–25).

At the conclusion of his homily, as Romero turned to the altar, a shot rang out. Moments earlier, a military sharpshooter had pulled up across the street. From the window of the car, he shot one bullet through the heart of the archbishop. Romero fell mortally wounded at the altar, the religious sisters and hospital patients running to his aid. They

---

1. James Brockman, *Romero: A Life* (Orbis Books, 1989), 233.

rushed him to the nearby hospital, where he died within minutes.

Romero's final homily remains a fitting testament to his own witness and to thousands of others. Here he places the struggle for peace and justice within the ultimate perspective of Christian hope. Amid all the struggles of life, the Christian is inspired and sustained by the hope of God's final reign, by the hope that God will indeed make all things new and resplendent with life. Romero emphasizes, "We know that every effort to improve society, especially when justice and sin are so widespread, is an effort that God blesses, that God wants, that God requires of us." The key, Romero says, is to infuse our work for peace and justice with true faith, hope, and love; such work then becomes like a seed of the kingdom, which can grow and blossom even here on earth.

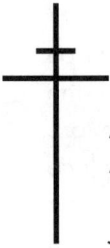

Monday, March 24, 1980
Mass Readings
1 Corinthians 15:20–28; Psalm 23:1–4
John 12:23–26

Because of what Jorgito has written in today's editorial in *El Independiente*, I have been able to enter into his filial sentiments on this anniversary of his mother's death, and I have especially been able to appreciate the noble spirit of Doña Sarita, who dedicated all her cultural formation and graciousness to the service of a cause that is so necessary today: the true liberation of our people.

This afternoon, dear sisters and brothers, I believe we should not only pray for the eternal rest of our dear Sarita but should above all embrace this message that every Christian today must heartily proclaim. Many people don't understand the message. They think that Christianity should not get involved in these things, but quite the opposite is true. You just heard the Gospel of Christ: we must not love our lives so much that we avoid taking the risks in life that history calls for. Those who seek to shun danger will lose their lives, whereas those who for love of Christ dedicate themselves to the service of others will live. They are like that grain of wheat that dies, at least in appearance. If the grain does not die, it remains alone (John 12:24–25). If it yields a crop, it is because it dies, allowing itself to be immolated in the earth; it is by being dismantled that it produces the crop.

From her place in eternity Doña Sarita can give us marvelous confirmation of this text I have chosen for her from the Second Vatican Council:

We do not know the time for the consummation of the earth and of humanity, nor do we know how all things will be transformed. As deformed by sin, the shape of this world will pass away; but we are taught that God is preparing a new dwelling place and a new earth where justice will abide, and whose blessedness will answer and surpass all the longings for peace which spring up in the human heart. Then, with death overcome, the sons and daughters of God will be raised up in Christ, and what was sown in weakness and corruption will be invested with incorruptibility. Enduring with charity and its fruits, all that creation which God made on humanity's account will be unchained from the bondage of vanity.

Therefore, while we are warned that it profits us nothing if we gain the whole world and lose ourselves, the expectation of a new earth must not weaken but rather stimulate our concern for cultivating this one. For here grows the body of a new human family, a body which even now is able to give some kind of foreshadowing of the new age.

Hence, while earthly progress must be carefully distinguished from the growth of Christ's kingdom, to the extent that the former can contribute to the better ordering of human society, it is of vital concern to the kingdom of God. For after we have obeyed the Lord, and in his Spirit nurtured on earth the values of human dignity, fraternity, and freedom, and indeed all the good fruits of our nature and enterprise, we will find them again, but freed of stain, burnished and transfigured, when Christ hands over to the Father "a kingdom eternal and universal, a kingdom of truth and life, of holiness and grace, of justice, love and peace." On this earth that kingdom is already present in mystery. When the Lord returns it will be brought into full flower. (*Gaudium et Spes* 39)

This is the hope that inspires us as Christians. We know that every effort to improve society, especially when injustice and sin are so widespread, is an effort that God blesses, that God wants, that God requires of us. We give thanks when we encounter people as generous as Doña Sarita and when we see her ideals reflected in Jorgito and all those who work for the same ideals. Of course, we must purify them in Christianity and invest them with hope for what lies beyond because in that way they become stronger. For we have the assurance that we will never fail in all the work we do on earth if we infuse it with Christian hope. We will find it purified in that kingdom where our merit will be according to what we have done on this earth.

I believe that on this anniversary we must aspire to live by her spirit of hope and of struggle. We remember with gratitude this woman who could understand the concerns of her husband, her son, and all those who are working for a better world. She also did her part, sowing her grain of wheat in suffering. There can be no doubt that her place in heaven will be in proportion to her spirit of sacrifice and comprehension, a spirit that is lacking in many people at this time in El Salvador.

I ask all of you, dear brothers and sisters, to view these things that are happening in our historical moment with a spirit of hope, generosity, and sacrifice. And let us do what we can. We can all do something and be more understanding. This holy woman whom we are remembering today perhaps could not do anything directly, but she encouraged those who were doing something, she understood their struggle, and she above all prayed. Even after death she speaks to us a message from eternity, telling us that our work is worthwhile. If we illuminate with Christian hope our intense longings for justice and peace and all that is good, then we can be sure that no one dies forever. If we have imbued our work with a sense of great faith, love of God, and hope for humanity, then all our endeavors will lead to the splendid crown that is the sure reward for the work of sowing truth, justice, love, and goodness on earth. Our work does not remain here; it is gathered and purified by the Spirit of God and returned to us as a reward.

This holy Mass of thanksgiving, then, is just such an act of faith. By Christian faith we know that at this moment the host of wheat becomes the body of the Lord who offered himself for the redemption of the world, and that the wine in this chalice is transformed into the blood that was the price of salvation. May this body that was immolated and this flesh that was sacrificed for humankind also nourish us so that we can give our bodies and our blood to suffering and pain, as Christ did, not for our own sake but to bring justice and peace to our people. Let us therefore join closely together in faith and hope at this moment of prayer for Doña Sarita and ourselves.

[At that moment, a shot rang out.]

Conclusion

Óscar Romero experienced the way the prophet is all at once embraced, beloved, slandered, and rejected. And, for him, this was true both in life and in death. The poor and the oppressed of El Salvador immediately declared him a saint with their veneration, images, and songs. His opponents claimed he had been nothing but a pawn of the Marxist left. His funeral was a microcosm of this division. Thousands of people gathered in the cathedral square, joined by hundreds of bishops, theologians, and leaders from around the world. But the majority of the Salvadoran bishops did not attend. And midway through the funeral Mass, shots rang out and chaos ensued. Romero's body was rushed inside. The Mass unfinished, Romero's body was buried in the cathedral. That unfinished Mass is a fitting symbol of Romero's service to a true peace and liberation for his people.

Following his death came twelve years of brutal civil war. In that time, it is estimated that more than seventy-five thousand people, mostly innocent civilians, were killed in the violence. Embraced by millions of Christians around the world and within El Salvador, Romero remained controversial in his country and in his Church. Lifted up as an inspiration by the revolutionary forces, conservative sectors of the society and Church avoided or maligned his witness. When John Paul II visited El Salvador in 1983, he was told by his advisors that he should not visit Romero's tomb—it would be too controversial. It is hard to imagine another case where the tomb of a martyred bishop, killed while celebrating Mass, not only would not be central to the pope's visit, but be avoided altogether. To his credit, the pope ignored his advisors and took a detour to pray publicly before Romero's body. Yet, within the Vatican, several cardinals continued to work for decades to delay Romero's cause for canonization. After nearly forty years of doctrinal assessments and reassessments, investigations, and testimonies, Romero was officially canonized a saint on October 14, 2018.

Romero's witness remains an inspiration and a challenge today. A true saint reveals something essential of what it means to be a disciple of Jesus and true servant of the kingdom of God. The saint, in their unique and unrepeatable life, illumines each of our particular journeys. Romero's life points to God's love of the poor, to solidarity as our path, and to true peace as our goal. But how exactly we receive this witness—what it demands of each of us—is our own responsibility. Romero insisted on this in his account of his preaching: "My preaching should not be the same here in El Salvador as it would be in Africa or at some other time in history." Romero believed that the Living Word speaks powerfully and distinctly into the particularities of each time, place, and life. So too the witness of Saint Óscar Romero. If it is to be a *living* witness, it is *our* task to receive it with humility, gratitude, and, ultimately, responsibility.

Further Reading

Romero's homilies as archbishop—the Spanish transcriptions, English translations, and often the original audio—are available free online through the Archbishop Romero Trust ((http://www.romerotrust.org.uk). The homilies are also published in English under the title, *A Prophetic Bishop Speaks to His People: The Complete Homilies of Archbishop Óscar Arnulfo Romero*, 6 vols., trans. Joseph Owens, SJ (Convivium Press, 2015–2016). Smaller selections from Romero's preaching are found in a number of books, including *The Violence of Love*, ed. James Brockman (Orbis Books, 2004) and *Through the Year with Oscar Romero: Daily Meditations*, trans. Irene B. Hodgson (Franciscan Media, 2015).

Romero's pastoral letters are collected in *Voice of the Voiceless: The Four Pastoral Letters and Other Statements*, trans. Michael J. Walsh (Orbis Books, 1985). His audio diary from the last two years of his life is published in *A Shepherd's Diary*, trans. Irene B. Hodgson (St. Anthony Messenger Press, 1993). These texts are also accessible online at the Romero Trust website.

The standard biography of Romero remains James Brockman, *Romero: A Life* (Orbis Books, 1989). For a shorter biography with wonderful pictures throughout, see Scott Wright, *Oscar Romero and the Communion of Saints* (Orbis Books, 2009). Another recent biography is Roberto Morozzo della Rocca, *Óscar Romero: Prophet of Hope* (DTL, 2015). Finally, a wonderful collection of testimonials and memories of those who knew Romero can be found in María López Vigil, *Monseñor Romero: Memories in Mosaic* (Orbis Books, 2013).

There are an increasing number of academic works on Romero's theology. I would initially recommend four books: Edgardo Colón-Emeric, *Óscar Romero's Theological Vision: Liberation and the Transfiguration of the Poor* (University of Notre Dame Press, 2018), Michael E. Lee, *Revolutionary Saint: The Theological Legacy of Óscar Romero* (Orbis Books, 2018), Matthew Whelan, *Blood in the Fields: Óscar Romero, Catholic Social Teaching, and Land Reform* (Catholic University of America Press, 2020), and Todd Walatka, ed., *Óscar Romero and Catholic Social Teaching* (University of Notre Dame Press, 2024).